30	trente trahı
31	trente-et-un trahN-teh-aN
32	trente-deux trahNt-duh
40	quarante kah-rahNt
50	cinquante saNk-ahNt
60	soixante swah-sahNt
70	soixante-dix swah-sahNt-deess
80	quatre-vingts kah-truh-vaN
90	quatre-vingt dix kah-truh-vaN deess
100	cent sahN
101	cent un sahNt-aN
102	cent deux sahN-duh
110	cent dix sahN-deess
111	cent onze sahNt-ohNz
120	cent vingt sahN-vaN
200	deux cent duh sahN
300	trois cent trwah sahN
400	quatre cent kah-truh sahN
437	quatre cent trente-sept kah-truh-sahN-trahNt-set
1000	mille meel
2000	deux mille duh meel
10.000	dix mille dee meel
100.000	cent mille sahN meel
1.000.000	un million aN meel-yohN

The Basics

Good afternoon!	Bonjour! bohN-zhoor
Good evening!	Bonsoir! bohN-swahr
Goodbye!	Au revoir. oh-ruh-vwah
…, please!	…, s'il vous plaît. see voo play
Thank you.	Merci. mehr-see
Yes.	Oui. wee
No.	Non. nohN
Sorry!	Excusez-moi. ex-kew-zeh-mwah
Get *a doctor / an ambulance*, quick!	Appelez vite *un médecin / une ambulance*! ah-play veet *aN mad-saN / ewn ahN-bew-lahN*s
Where are the restrooms?	Où sont les toilettes? oo sohN lay twah-let
When?	Quand? kahN
What?	Quoi? kwah
Where?	Où? oo
Here.	Ici. ee-see
There.	Là-bas lah bah
On the right.	À droite. ah drwaht
On the left.	À gauche. ah gohsh
Do you have …?	Avez-vous…? ah-veh-voo
I'd like …	J'aimerais bien… zhem-eh-reh bee-aN
How much is that?	Ça coûte combien? sah koot kohN-bee-aN
Where is …?	Où est…? oo eh
Where can I get …?	Où est-ce-qu'il y a…? oo es-keel yah

III

Langenscheidt

Pocket Phrasebook
French

with Travel Dictionary
and Grammar

Langenscheidt

Berlin·Munich·Vienna·Zurich·New York

Authors: Marie-France Cecchini, Magaly Baudel, Maria Hoffmann-Dartevell
Graphic Design: Kathrin Mosandl
Editorial: Emily Bernath, Juergen Lorenz, Bert Weaver

Photo Credits:
APA Publications: p. 24, 30, 59; Corbis images: p. 13; E. Sagenschneider:
p. 30, 39, 49, 54, 103, 109, 116, 169; John Fox Images: p. 79; MEV: p. 19,
23, 63, 64, 73, 137, 141, 162, 175, 181, 193, 203; Photodisc: p, 37, 77,
114, 156, 199; Stockbyte: p. 69, 206, 120

ISBN 1-58573-507-8
Printed in Germany
www.langenscheidt.com

Table of Contents

Travel with Children _____ 63

For the Disabled _____ 69

Communications _____ 73

Eating and Drinking _____ 77

Table of Contents

Shopping _____ 103

Sports and Leisure   137

Things to Do   153

Money, Mail and Police   169

Table of Contents

When different gender forms apply, the masculine form will be indicated by ♂, the feminine form by ♀. Therefore, a man would say: Je suis ♂ heureux. A woman would say: Je suis ♀ heureuse.

Bye!	Salut! sah-lew
It was nice meeting you.	Je suis ♂ heureux / ♀ heureuse d'avoir fait votre / ta connaissance. zhuh swee uhr-uh / uhr-uhz dah-vwah feh vo-truh / tah cohN-nay-sahns
Thank you for a lovely *evening / day*.	Merci pour cette charmante *soirée / journée*. mehr-see poor set shahr-mahNt swah-ray / zhoor-nay

The pronunciation of each word is given. Simply read it as if it were an English word. See also simplified pronunciation guide pages 10-12.

Sometimes you see two alternatives in italics, separated by a slash. Choose the one that is appropriate for the situation, e.g. soirée for evening or journée for day.

yourself? Comme va? koh

What's your name? Comment *vous appelez-vous / tu t'appelles*? koh-mahN voo-zah-play voo / tew-tah-pel

French has a formal (form.) and informal (inform.) way to address people. See also grammar section page 204.

How to Use This Book

The arrow indicates
where you find additional
expressions.

If there is more
than one way
to continue a
sentence, any
of the possibili-
ties that follow
can be inserted.

► *Accepting / Declining an Invitation, page 22*

Where's the
nearest …

Où est … *le / la* p
… *luh / lah* plew p

— subway station?

— la station de métro lah stah-see-
ohN duh may-troh

— bus stop?

— l'arrêt d'autobus lah-ray-do-toh-
bewss

Which *bus / subway* goes to
..?

Quel bus / quel métro va à …? *kel
bewss / kel may-tro vah ah*

Where is the bus stop to
..?

Où est l'arrêt d'autobus pour…? oo
eh lah-ray do-toh-bewss poor

Le bus numéro …

The bus number …

La ligne …

The … line.

Are there discounts for…?

Est-ce qu'il y a une réduction
pour …? es-keel ya ewn ray-dewk-see-
ohN poor

Do I have to transfer to get
to …?

Pour …, est-ce que je dois changer?
poor … es-kuh zhuh dwah shahN-zheh

Could you tell me where I

Pouv

You can insert
your choice of
word(s) from the
Additional Words
section in place of
ellipses marks.

dois
desc veh voo
mi

Phrases that you
may hear but may
never say are
shown in reverse,
with French on the
left side.

Pronunciation

This section is designed to make you familiar with the sounds of French. You'll find the pronunciation of the French letters and sounds explained below, together with their "imitated" equivalents. Simply read the pronunciation as if it were English, noting any special rules below.

Consonants

Letter	Approximate Pronunciation	Symbol	Example	Pronunciation
ch	like sh in shut	sh	chercher	shehrshay
ç	like s in sit	s	ça	sah
g	1) before e, i, y, like s in pleasure	zh	manger	mangzhay
	2) before a, o, u, like g in go	g	garçon	gahrsawN
gn	like ni in onion	n	ligne	leen
h	always silent		homme	om
j	like s in pleasure	zh	jamais	zhahmay
qu	like k in kill	k	qui	kee
r	rolled in the back of the mouth, like gargling	r	rouge	roozh
w	usually like v in voice	v	wagon	vahgawN

Vowels

a, à or â	between the a in hat and the a in father	a/ah	mari	mahree
é or ez	like a in late	ay	été	aytay
è, ê, e	like e in get	e/eh	même	mem
e	sometimes like er in other	er	je	zher
i	like ee in meet	ee	il	eel
o	generally like o in hot	o/oh	donner	donnay
ô	like o	o/oh	Rhône	rohn
u	like ew in dew	ew	cru	krew

Letters b, c, d, f, k, l, m, n, p, s, t, v, x and z are pronounced as in English.

Sounds spelled with two or more letters

Letter	Approximate Pronunciation	Symbol	Example	Pronunciation
ai, ay, aient,ais,	can be pronounced like *a* in late or	ay	j'ai vais	zhay vay
ait, aî, ei	like *e* in get	e/eh	chaîne peine	shen pen
(e)au	similar to o	o/oh	chaud	sho
eu, eû, œu	like *ur* in f*ur*, but with lips rounded, not spread	ur	peu	pur
euil, euille	like *uh* in h*uh*, but without pronouncing the *h* and with a *y* sound added	uhy	feuille	fuhy
ail, aille	like *ie* in t*ie*	ie	taille	tie
oi, oy	like w followed by the a in hat	wa	moi	mwah
ou, oû	like o in move or oo in hoot	oo	nouveau	noovo
ui	approximately like wee in between	wee	traduire	trahdweer

Nasal Sounds

French contains nasal vowels, which are transcribed with a vowel symbol plus N. This N should not be pronounced strongly but is included to show the nasal quality of the previous vowel. A nasal vowel is pronounced simultaneously through the mouth and the nose.

Liaison

Normally, final consonants of words are not pronounced in French. However, when a word ending in a consonant is followed by one beginning with a vowel, they are often run together, and the consonant is pronounced as if it began the following word.

Examples:

nous	*noo*
nous avons un enfant	*noo zavawN zaN nahngfahN*
comment	*komahN*
Comment allez-vous?	*komahN-tah-lay-voo*

Stress

All syllables in French are pronounced with more or less the same degree of stress (loudness). Stress has not been indicated in the phonetic transcription and each syllable should be pronounced with equal stress.

Pronunciation of the French Alphabet

A	ah		N	en
B	bay		O	o
C	say		P	pay
D	day		Q	kew
E	er		R	ehr
F	ef		S	ess
G	zhay		T	tay
H	ahsh		U	ew
I	ee		V	vay
J	zhee		W	dooblervay
K	kah		X	eex
L	el		Y	ee grek
M	em		Z	zed

Meeting People

How are you?
Comment allez-vous?

Fine, thanks.
Très bien, merci.

Communication Difficulties

Do you speak English?	Parlez-vous anglais? pah-lay voo ahN-glay
Does anyone here speak English?	Est-ce que quelqu'un ici parle anglais? es-kuh kel-kaN ee-see pahrl ahN-glay
Did you understand that?	Vous avez compris? vooz-ah-veh kohN-pree
I understand.	J'ai compris. zheh kohN-pree
I didn't understand that.	Je n'ai pas compris. zhuh nay pah kohN-pree
Could you speak a bit more slowly, please?	Vous pourriez parler un peu plus lentement, s'il vous plaît? voo poor-ee-eh pah-lay aN puh plew lahN-tuh-mahN see voo-play
Could you repeat that?	Vous pourriez répéter? voo poor-ee-eh ray-pay-teh
What does ... mean?	Que veut dire ...? kuh vuh deer
Could you write it down for me?	Vous pourriez me l'écrire? voo poor-ee-eh muh lay-creer

Greetings

Good morning / afternoon!	Bonjour! bohN-zhoor
Good evening!	Bonsoir! bohN-swah
Goodnight!	Bonne nuit! bun nwee
Hello!	Salut! sah-lew

14

info Greetings vary according to how well you know someone. It's polite to shake hands, both when you meet and say good-bye. Good friends sometimes give each other a hug, and women kiss each other on the cheeks.

How are you?	Comment allez-vous / vas-tu? koh-mahN-tah-lay-voo / vah-tew
How are things?	Comment ça va? koh-mahN sah-vah
Fine, thanks. And you?	Très bien, merci. Et vous? tray bee-aN mehr-see eh voo
I'm afraid I have to go now.	Je suis désolé, mais je dois partir maintenant. zhuh swee day-zo-lay may zhuh dwah pah-teer maN-tuh-nahN
Goodbye!	Au revoir! oh-ruh-vwah
See you *soon* / *tomorrow*!	A *bientôt* / *demain*! ah *bee-aN-toh* / *duh-maN*
Bye!	Salut! sah-lew
It was nice meeting you.	Je suis ♂ heureux / ♀ heureuse d'avoir fait votre connaissance. zhuh swee ♂ uhr-uh / ♀ uhr-uhz dah-vwah feh vo-truh kohN-nay-sahN
Thank you for a lovely *evening* / *day*.	Merci pour cette charmante *soirée* / *journée*. mehr-see poor set shahr-mahNt *swah-ray* / *zhoor-nay*
Have a good trip!	Bon voyage! bohN vwah-yazh

Getting to Know Each Other

Introductions

What's your name?	Comment *vous appelez-vous / tu t'appelles*? koh-mahN *voo-zah-play voo / tew-tah-pel*
My name is …	Je m'appelle … zhuh mah-pel
May I introduce …	Permettez-moi de vous présenter. C'est … pehr-met-teh-mwah duh voo pray-sahN-teh say
– my husband.	– mon mari. mohN mah-ree
– my wife.	– ma femme. mah fahm
– my (boy)friend.	– mon ami. mohN-nah-mee
– my (girl)friend.	– mon amie. mohN-nah-mee

Where are you from?	D'où *venez-vous / viens-tu*? doo *vuh-nay-voo / vee-aN tew*
I'm from …	Je viens … zhuh vee-aN
– the US.	– des États-Unis. day-zeh-tah-sew-nee
– Canada.	– du Canada. dew kah-nah-dah
– the UK.	– du Royaume-Uni. dew rwah-yohm-ew-nee

How old are you?	Quel âge *avez-vous* / *as-tu*? kel ahzh *ah-veh-voo* / *ah tew*
I'm …	J'ai … ans. zheh … ahN
Are you married?	*Êtes-vous* / *Es-tu* marié? *et-voo* / *eh-tew* mah-ree-eh
Do you have any children?	Avez-vous des enfants? ah-veh-voo day-zaN-fahN

Asking Someone Out

▶ *Accepting / Declining an Invitation, page 18*

Would you like to go out *tonight* / *tomorrow*?	Si on se voyait *ce soir* / *demain*? see ohN suh vwa-yeh *suh swah* / *duh-maN*
We could do something together, if you like.	On pourrait faire quelque chose ensemble, si vous le voulez. ohN poor-eh fehr kel-kuh shoze ahN-sahN-bluh see voo voo-lay
Would you like to have dinner together tonight?	Si on dînait ensemble ce soir? see ohN dee-nay ahN-sahN-bluh suh swah

▶ *Nightlife, page 167*

I'd like to take you out.	Je voudrais vous inviter. zhuh voo-dray voo-zaN-vee-teh
Would you like to go dancing?	Voulez-vous aller danser? voo-lay-voo ah-lay dahN-say
What time should we meet?	On se donne rendez-vous à quelle heure? ohN suh done rahN-day-voo ah kel uhr

Let's meet at …	Disons qu'on se rencontre à … heures. dee-zohn kohN suh rahN-kohN-truh ah … uhr
I'll take you home.	Je vous raccompagne jusque chez vous. zhuh voo rah-kohN-pahn-yuh zhews-kuh sheh voo
Could we meet again?	On va se revoir? ohN vah suh ruh-vwah

Accepting / Declining an Invitation

I'd love to.	Très volontiers. treh vol-ohN-teeyeh
OK.	O.K., d'accord. oh-keh dah-kaw
I don't know yet.	Je ne sais pas encore. zhuh nuh say pah-zahN-kaw
Maybe.	Peut-être. puh-tet-truh
I'm sorry, but I can't.	Je suis désolé, mais je ne peux pas. zhuh swee day-zo-lay may zhuh nuh puh pah
I'm already doing something.	J'ai déjà quelque chose de prévu. zheh day-zhah kel-kuh shoze duh pray-vew

Flirting and Romance

▶ Asking Someone Out, page 17

| Did you come by yourself? | Vous êtes ♂seul / ♀seule ici? voo-zet suhl ee-see |
| Do you have a boyfriend / girlfriend? | As-tu un ami / une amie? ah-tew aN-nah-mee / ew-nah-mee |

18

You're very beautiful.	Tu es magnifique. tew eh mahnee-fee-kuh
I like you.	Je t'aime bien. zhuh tem-bee-aN
I love you.	Je t'aime. zhuh tem
Are you coming back to my place?	Tu viens chez moi? tew vee-aN sheh mwah
Leave me alone!	Laissez-moi tranquille! lay-say mwah traN-kee

Polite Expressions

Expressing Likes and Dislikes

Very good!	Très bien! treh bee-aN
I'm very happy.	Je suis très ♂ content / ♀ contente. zhuh swee treh ♂ kohN-taN / ♀ kohN-taNt
I like that.	Ça me plaît. sah-muh-play
What a shame!	Dommage! doh-mazh

I'd rather …	J'aimerais mieux …
	zhem-eh-reh myuh
I don't like it.	Ça ne me plaît pas.
	sahn nuh muh play pah
I'd rather not.	Je ne préfèrerais pas.
	zhuh nuh pray-fehr-eh pah
Certainly not.	En aucun cas. ahN oh-kaN kah

Expressing Requests and Thanks

Thank you very much.	Merci beaucoup. mehr-see bo-koo
May I?	Vous permettez? voo pehr-met-teh
Please, …	S'il vous plaît, … see-voo-play
No, thank you.	Non, merci. nohN mehr-see
Could you help me, please?	Est-ce que vous pourriez m'aider, s'il vous plaît? es-kuh voo poor-ee-eh meh-day see-voo-play
Thank you. That's very nice of you.	Merci beaucoup. C'est très aimable de votre part. mehr-see bo-koo seh treh-zem-ah-bluh duh vo-truh pah
You're welcome.	Il n'y a pas de quoi. eel nee-ah pahd-kwah

Apologies

Sorry!	Pardon! pahr-dohN
Excuse me!	Excusez-moi! ex-kew-say mwah
I'm sorry about that.	Je suis désolé. zhuh swee day-zo-lay

Don't worry about it!	Ça ne fait rien! sahn nuh feh ree-aN
How embarrassing!	C'est très embarrassant pour moi! seh treh-zahN-bah-rahs-sahN poor mwah
It was a misunderstanding.	C'était un malentendu. say-teh aN mah-lahN-tahn-dew

Meeting People: Additional Words

address	l'adresse *f* lah-dress
alone	seul suhl
to be called; my name is	s'appeler; je m'appelle sah-play; zhuh mah-pel
to be from	venir de vuh-neer duh
boy	le garçon luh gah-sohN
boyfriend	l'ami *m* lah-mee
brother	le frère luh frehr
brothers and sisters	les frères et sœurs *m/pl* lay-frehr eh suhr
child	l'enfant *m* lahN-fahN
to come back	revenir ruh-vuh-neer
country	le pays luh pay-ee
daughter	la fille la fee
engaged	fiancé fee-ahN-say
father	le père luh pehr
free	libre lee-bruh
friend	l'amie *f* lah-mee
friend	l'ami *m* lah-mee
girl	la jeune fille lah zhuhn fee
girlfriend	l'amie *f* lah-mee
to go dancing	aller danser ah-lay dahN-say
to go out to eat	aller manger ah-lay mahN-zheh
husband	le mari luh mah-ree

21

to invite	inviter aN-vee-teh
to like	aimer em-eh
to make a date	se donner rendez-vous
	suh dun-nay rahN-day-voo
married	marié mah-ree-eh
to meet	faire la connaissance de
	fehr lah koh-nay-sahNs duh
to meet	se rencontrer suh rahN-kohN-tray
mother	la mère lah mehr
Mr.	Monsieur muh-syuh
Ms.	Madame ma-dahm
partner	le compagnon / la compagne luh
	kohN-pahn-yohN / la kohN-pahn-yuh
photo	la photo lah fo-toh
please	s'il vous plaît see voo-play
to repeat	répéter ray-pay-teh
school	l'école *f* lay-cuhl
sister	la sœur lah suhr
slowly	lentement lahN-tuh-mahN
son	le fils luh feess
to speak	parler pah-lay
student	l'étudiant / l'étudiante
	lay-tew-dyahN / lay-tew-dyahNt
to study	faire des études fehr day-zeh-tewd
thank you	merci mehr-see
to understand	comprendre kohN-prahN-druh
vacation	les vacances *f/pl* lay vah-kahNs
to wait	attendre ah-tahN-druh
wife	la femme la fahm

Accommodations

Where's the tourist information office?
Où se trouve l'office du tourisme?

The key to room ..., please.
La clé de la chambre ..., s'il vous plaît.

Lodging

Looking for a Room

Where's the tourist information office?	Où se trouve l'office du tourisme? oo suh troov law-feess dew toor-eez-muh
Can you recommend …	Vous pourriez me recommander … voo poor-ee-eh muh ruh-kohN-mahN-day
– a good hotel?	– un bon hôtel? aN bohn o-tel
– a reasonably priced hotel?	– un hôtel pas trop cher? aN-no-tel pah tro shehr
– a bed & breakfast?	– une pension? ewn pahN-see-ohN
Could you make a reservation for me?	Vous pourriez réserver pour moi? voo poor-ee-eh ray-sehr-veh poor mwah
Is it far from here?	C'est loin d'ici? say lwahN dee-see

HÔTEL DU POULDU

How do I get there?	Comment est-ce que je peux m'y rendre? koh-mahN es kuh zhuh puh mee rahN-druh

Arriving

I have a reservation. My name is …	On a retenu chez vous une chambre à mon nom. Je m'appelle … ohN ah ruh-ten-ew sheh voo ewn shahN-bruh ah mohN nohN zhuh mahpell
Do you have a *double* / *single* room …	Vous auriez une chambre pour *deux personnes* / *une personne* … voo-zoh-ree-eh ewn shahN-bruh poor *duh pehr-sun* / *ewn pehr-sun*
– for one night?	– pour une nuit? poor ewn nwee
– for … nights?	– pour … nuits? poor … nwee
– with a bathroom?	– avec salle de bains? ah-vek sahl-duh-baN
– with a balcony?	– avec balcon? ah-vek bahl-kohN
– with air conditioning?	– avec climatisation? ah-vek klee-mah-tee-zah-see-ohN
– with a fan?	– avec un ventilateur? ah-vek vahN-tee-lah-tuhr
– with an ocean view?	– avec vue sur la mer? ah-vek vew sewr lah mehr

info All types of accommodations can be found through the Office du Tourisme / Syndicat d'initiative, the tourist information center.

Malheureusement, nous sommes complets.	I'm afraid we're booked.

How much is it …	Combien ça coûte … kohN-bee-aN sah koot
– with breakfast?	– avec le petit déjeuner? ah-vek luh puh-tee day-zhuhn-eh
– without breakfast?	– sans le petit déjeuner? sahN luh puh-tee day-zhuhn-eh
– with breakfast and lunch or dinner?	– avec la demi-pension? ah-vek lah duh-mee pahN-see-ohN
– with all meals included?	– avec la pension complète? ah-vek lah pahN-see-ohN kohN-plet
Do you offer a discount if I stay … nights?	Est-ce qu'il y a une réduction, si l'on reste … nuits? es-keel-yah ewn ray-dewk-see-ohN see lohN rest … nwee

▶ *Numbers, see inside front cover*

Can I see the room?	Je pourrais voir la chambre? zhuh poor-eh vwah lah shahN-bruh
Could you put in an extra bed?	Vous pourriez installer un lit supplémentaire? voo poor-ee-eh aN- stah-lay aN lee sew-pluh-mahN-tehr
Do you have another room?	Vous auriez encore une autre chambre? voo-zo-ree-eh ahN-kaw ewn o-truh shahN-bruh
It's very nice. I'll take it.	Elle me plaît. Je la prends. el muh play zhuh lah prahN
Could you take my luggage up to the room?	Vous pourriez apporter mes bagages dans la chambre? voo poor- ee-eh ahp-paw-teh may bah-gahzh dahN lah shahN-bruh

26

Where's the bathroom?
Où sont les toilettes?
oo sohN lay twah-let

Where can I park my car?
Où est-ce que je peux garer ma voiture? oo es kuh zhuh puh gah-ray mah vwah-tewr

Between what hours is breakfast served?
Jusqu'á quelle heure est servi le petit déjeuner? zhews-kah kel huhr eh sehr-vee luh puh-tee day-zhuh-nay

Where's the dining room?
Où est la salle à manger?
oo eh lah sahl ah mahN-zheh

Service

Can I leave my valuables with you for safekeeping?
Est-ce que je peux vous confier mes objets de valeur? es kuh zhuh puh voo kohN-fee-eh may-zob-zheh duh vah-luhr

I'd like to pick up my valuables.
Je voudrais reprendre mes objets de valeur. zhuh voo-dreh ruh-praN-druh may-zob-zheh duh vah-luhr

The key to room ..., please.
La clé de la chambre ..., s'il vous plaît. lah clay duh lah shahN-bruh ... see voo play

Can I call the *US/UK* from my room?
Est-ce que je peux téléphoner *aux États-Unis / en Grande-Bretagne* de ma chambre? es kuh zuh puh tel-eh-foh-nay *o-zeh-tah-zew-nee / ahN grand-bruh-tahn* duh mah shahN-bruh

Are there any messages for me?
Est-ce qu'il y a un message pour moi? es keel-yah aN mes-sahzh poor mwah

Could I have …, please?	Est-ce que je peux avoir…, s'il vous plaît? es kuh zhuh puh ah-vwah … see-voo-play
– an extra blanket	– une couverture supplementaire ewn koo-vehr-tewr sew-pluh-mahN-tehr
– an extra towel	– une serviette supplementaire ewn sehr-vee-et sew-pluh-mahN-tehr
– a few more hangers	– quelques porte-vêtements supplementaires kel-kuh pawt-vet-mahN sew-pluh-mahN-tehr
– an extra pillow	– un autre oreiller aN o-truh aw-ray-eh
The window won't *open* / *close*.	La fenêtre ne *s'ouvre* / *ferme* pas. lah fuh-net-ruh nuh *soo-vruh* / *fehrm* pah
… doesn't work.	… ne marche pas. nuh mahsh pah
– The shower	– La douche lah doosh
– The TV	– La télévision lah teh-lay-vee-see-ohN

– The heat	– Le chauffage luh sho-fahzh
– The Internet connection	– La connexion à Internet lah koh-nek-see-ohN ah aN-tehr-net
– The air conditioning	– La climatisation lah klee-mah-tee-zah-see-ohN
– The light	– La lumière lah lewm-yehr

The *drain / toilet* is clogged.

Le lavabo est bouché. / Les toilettes sont bouchées. luh lah-vah-bo eh boo-sheh / lay twah-let sohN boo-sheh

… is dirty.

… est sale. eh sahl

Departure

Please wake me at … (tomorrow morning).	Réveillez-moi (demain matin) à … heures, s'il vous plaît. ray-feh-yeh-mwah (duh-maN mah-taN) ah … uhr see-voo-play
We're leaving tomorrow.	Nous partons demain. noo pah-tohN duh-maN
May I have my bill, please?	Préparez-nous la note, s'il vous plaît. prey-pah-ray-noo lah note see-voo-play
It was very nice here.	Nous avons passé un séjour très agréable. noo-zah-vohN pahss-eh aN say-zhoor treh-zah-gray-ah-bluh
Can I leave my luggage here until …?	Est-ce que je peux encore laisser mes bagages ici jusqu'à … heures? es kuh zhuh puh ahN-kaw less-eh may bah-gahzh ee-see zhuhsk-ah…uhr
Please call me a taxi.	Appelez-moi un taxi, s'il vous plaît. ah-play-mwah aN tahx-ee see voo play

29

Rentals

We've rented apartment …	Nous avons loué l'appartement … noo-zah-vohN loo-eh lah-paht-uh-mahN
Je pourrais avoir votre bon de réservation?	Could I have your coupon / voucher, please?
Where do we get the keys?	Où pouvons-nous prendre les clés? oo poo-vohN-noo prahN-druh lay clay

info The 220-volt / 50-cycle AC is universal in France, Belgium, and Switzerland. Buy an adapter with round, not square, pins if you bring electrical appliances. If they cannot be switched to 220 volts you'll also need a transformer appropriate to the wattage of the appliance.

Accommodations

Could we please have some (extra) *bed linens / dish towels*?

Nous pourrions avoir *des draps / des torchons* (en plus)? noo poor-ee-ohN ah-vwah *day drah / day taw-shohN* (ahN plews)

Could you show us how … works, please?

Vous pourriez nous expliquer comment fonctionne …, s'il vous plaît? voo poor-ee-eh noo-zex-plee-keh kohN-mahN fohNk-see-un … see-voo-play

– the dishwasher
– the stove
– the washing machine
– the dryer

– le lave-vaisselle luh lahv-veh-sel
– la cuisinière lah kwee-zeen-yehr
– la machine à laver lah mah-sheen ah lah-veh
– le séchoir luh say-shwahr

Where does the garbage go?

Où devons-nous déposer les ordures? oo duh-vohN-noo day-po-zeh lay-zaw-dewr

Where's …

Où se trouve … oo suh troov

– the nearest bus stop?
– a supermarket?

– a bakery?

– le prochain arrêt de l'autobus? luh pro-shaN ah-reh duh lo-to-bewss
– un supermarché? aN sew-pehr-mahr-sheh
– une boulangerie? ewn boo-lahN-zheh-ree

Camping

Is there room for …?

Est-ce qu'il y a encore de la place pour…? es keel yah ahN-kaw duh lah plahss poor

31

How much is it for …

– … adults and … children?
– a car with a trailer?

– an RV (recreational vehicle)?
– a tent?

Do you also rent out *bungalows / trailers*?

We'd like to stay for *one day / … days*.

Where can we *put up our tent / park our trailer*?

Where are the *bathrooms / restrooms*?

Where can I empty the chemical toilet?

Is there an electric hookup?

Quel est le tarif pour …
kel eh luh tah-reef poor

– … adultes et … enfants?
   … ah-dewlt eh … ahN-fahN
– une voiture avec caravane?
   ewn vwah-tewr ah-vek kah-rah-vahn
– un camping-car?
   aN kahN-ping kah
– une tente? ewn tahNt

Est-ce que vous louez aussi des *bungalows / caravanes*? es kuh voo loo-eh o-see day *bahN-gah-lo / cah-rah-vahn*

Nous voudrions rester *un jour / … jours*. noo voo-dree-ohN res-teh *aN zhoor / … zhoor*

Où pouvons-nous installer *notre tente / notre caravane*? oo poo-vohN-noo aN-stah-lay *no-truh tahNt / no-truh kah-rah-vahn*

Où sont les *lavabos / toilettes*? oo sohN lay *lah-vah-bo / twah-let*

Où est-ce que je peux vider les toilettes chimiques? oo es-kuh zhuh puh vee-day lay twah-let shee-meek

Vous avez un branchement électrique? voo-zah-veh aN brahNsh-mahN eh-lek-treek

Can I *buy* / *exchange* propane tanks here?	Je peux *acheter* / *échanger* des bouteilles de butane ici? zhuh puh *ahsh-teh* / *eh-shahN-zheh* day boo-teh duh bew-tahn ee-see

▶ Rentals, page 30

Accommodations: Additional Words

adapter	l'adaptateur *m* lah-dahp-tah-tuhr
advance booking	la réservation lah ray-sehr-vah-see-ohN
apartment	le studio luh stew-dyoh
armchair	le fauteuil luh fo-tuh-yuh
ashtray	le cendrier luh sahN-dree-eh
bathtub	la baignoire lah behn-wah
bed	le lit luh lee
bed linen	les draps *m/pl* lay drah
bedspread	la couverture lah koo-vehr-tewr
bill	la facture lah fahk-tewr
breakfast room	la salle du petit déjeuner lah sahl dew puh-tee day-zhuh-nay
broken	cassé kah-say
broom	le balai luh bah-lay
bulb	l'ampoule *f* lahN-pool
bunk beds	les lits *m/pl* superposés lay lee sew-pehr-po-say
to camp	camper kahN-per
camping	le camping luh kahN-ping
campsite	le terrain de camping luh tehr-aN duh kahN-ping
chair	la chaise lah shehz
check-in	la déclaration de séjour lah day-clah-rah-see-ohN duh say-zhoor

cleaning products	les produits *m/pl* de nettoyage
	lay pro-dwee duh neh-twhah-yazh
coffee-maker	la cafetière (électrique)
	lah kah-feh-tyehr (eh-lek-treek)
complaint	la réclamation
	lah ray-klah-mah-see-ohN
cot (for a child)	le lit d'enfant luh lee dahN-fahN
deposit	l'acompte *m* lah-kohNt
deposit	la caution lah ko-see-ohN
detergent	la lessive lah less-eev
dirty	sale sahl
dishes	la vaisselle lah veh-sel
dormitory	le dortoir luh daw-twah
double bed	le lit conjugal
	luh lee kohN-zhew-gahl
drain	l'écoulement lay-kool-mahN
drinking water	l'eau *f* potable lo po-tah-bluh
dryer	le sèche-linge luh sehsh-laNzh
elevator	l'ascenseur *m* lah-sahN-suhr
emergency exit	la sortie de secours
	lah sor-tee duh suh-koor
extension cord	la rallonge électrique
	lah rah-lohNzh eh-lek-treek
extra week	la semaine supplémentaire
	lah suh-men sew-pluh-mahN-tehr
faucet	le robinet luh raw-bee-neh
fireplace	la cheminée lah shuh-mee-nay
firewood	le bois de chauffage
	luh bwah duh sho-fahzh
floor	l'étage *m* lay-tazh
foam mattress	le tapis de sol luh tah-pee duh sol
fuse	le fusible luh few-zee-bluh
garbage can	la poubelle lah poo-bel
gas canister	la cartouche de gaz
	lah kah-toosh duh gahz

gas stove	le réchaud à gaz luh ray-sho ah gahz
glass	le verre luh vehr
hammer	le marteau luh mahr-to
hanger	le cintre luh saN-truh
to iron	repasser ruh-pah-say
lamp	la lampe lah lahNp
laundry room	les lavabos *m/pl* lay lah-vah-bo
to leave	partir pah-teer
lobby	le hall d'entrée luh ahl dahN-tray
lounge	la salle de réunion
	lah sahl duh ray-ewn-yohN
to make reservations	réserver ray-sehr-veh
mattress	le matelas luh maht-lah
minibar	le minibar luh mee-nee-bah
mirror	la glace lah glahss
mosquito coil	la spirale anti-moustiques
	lah spee-rahl ahN-tee-moo-steek
mosquito net	la moustiquaire lah moos-tee-kehr
off-peak season	la basse saison lah bahss say-sohN
outlet	la prise (de courant)
	lah preez (duh koo-rahN)
peak season	la haute saison lah oht say-sohN
phone	le téléphone luh tel-eh-fohn
plug	la fiche lah feesh
range	la cuisinière lah kwee-seen-yehr
reception	la réception lah ray-sep-see-ohN
refrigerator	le réfrigérateur
	luh ray-free-zheh-ah-tuhr
rent	le loyer luh lwah-yeh
to rent	louer loo-eh
rental fee	le prix de la location
	luh pree duh lah lo-kah-see-ohN
reserved	réservé ray-sehr-veh
room	la chambre lah shahN-bruh
RV (recreational vehicle)	le camping-car luh kahN-ping kah

safe	le coffre-fort luh kawf-ruh for
sheet	le drap luh drah
single bed	le lit à une place
	luh lee ah ewn plahss
sink	le lavabo luh lah-vah-bo
sleeping bag	le sac de couchage
	luh sahk duh-koo-shahzh
stove	le réchaud luh ray-sho
swimming pool	la piscine lah pee-seen
table	la table lah tah-bluh
tent	la tente lah tahNt
tent peg	le piquet (de tente)
	luh pee-keh (duh tahNt)
terrace	la terrasse lah teh-rahss
toilet paper	le papier hygiénique
	luh pah-pyeh ew-zhen-eek
toilet / restroom	les toilettes *f/pl* lay twah-let
trailer	la caravane lah kah-rah-vahn
TV room	la salle de télévision
	lah sahl duh teh-lay-vee-see-ohN
vacation home	la maison de vacances
	lah may-sohN duh vah-kahNs
voltage	le voltage luh vol-tahzh
wardrobe	l'armoire *f* lahr-mwah
washing machine	la machine à laver
	lah mah-sheen ah lah-veh
water	l'eau *f* lo
window	la fenêtre lah fuh-net-ruh
youth hostel	l'auberge *f* de jeunesse
	lo-behrzh duh zhuh-ness
youth hostel ID	la carte d'adhérent des auberges
	de jeunesse la kahrt dah-dehr-rahN
	day-zo-behrzh duh zhuh-ness

Travel

Excuse me, where's …?
Pardon, où est …?

Is this seat taken?
Est-ce que cette place est occupée?

Asking for Directions

Excuse me, where's …?	Pardon, où est …? pah-dohN oo eh
How do I get to …?	Pour aller à …? poor ah-lay ah
Could you please show me on the map?	Vous pouvez me le montrer sur la carte, s'il vous plaît? voo poo-veh muh luh mohN-treh sewr lah kahrt see voo play
How many minutes *on foot / by car*?	C'est à combien de minutes *à pied / en voiture*? say ah kohN-bee-aN duh mee-newt *ah pyeh / ahN vwah-tewr*
Is this the road to …?	C'est bien la route pour …? say bee-aN lah root poor
How do I get onto the expressway to …?	Comment arriver sur l'autoroute pour …? kohN-mahN ah-ree-veh sewr lo-toh-root poor
Je suis désolé, je ne sais pas.	I'm afraid I don't know.
La *première / deuxième* rue à *gauche / droite*.	The *first / second* road on your *left / right*.
Au prochain *feu / croisement* …	At the next *traffic light / intersection* …
Traversez *la place / la rue* …	Cross the *square / street* …
Vous pouvez prendre *le bus / le métro*.	You can take the *bus / subway*.

Where Is It?

à côté de	beside / next to
à droite	right / to the right
à gauche	left / to the left
assez loin	quite a long way
croisement *m*, carrefour *m*	intersection
derrière	after / behind
devant	before / in front of
en arrière	back
en bas de l'escalier	down the steps
en face de	opposite
en haut de l'escalier	up the steps
feu *m*	traffic lights
ici	here
là-bas	there
la rue	street
la route	road
par ici	this way
par là	over there
pas loin	not far
près de	nearby
tout droit	straight ahead
virage *m*	bend

Luggage / Baggage

I'd like to leave my luggage here.	Je voudrais laisser mes bagages ici. zhuh voo-dray less-eh may bah-gahzh ee-see
My luggage hasn't arrived (yet).	Mes bagages ne sont pas (encore) arrivés. may bah-gahzh nuh sohN pah (zahN-kaw) ah-ree-veh
Where's my luggage?	Où sont mes bagages? oo sohN may bah-gahzh
My suitcase has been damaged.	Ma valise a été abîmée. mah vah-leez ah eh-teh ah-bee-may
Whom should I speak to?	A qui est-ce que je peux m'adresser? ah kee-es-kuh zhuh puh mah-dress-eh

At the Airport

Where's the … desk?	Où est le guichet de la compagnie aérienne …? oo eh luh gee-sheh duh lah kohN-pahn-yee ah-ehr-ee-en
How much is a flight to …?	Combien coûte un vol pour …? kohN-bee-aN koot aN vol poor
A … ticket, please.	Un billet …, s'il vous plaît. aN bee-yeh… see voo play
– one-way	– aller simple ah-lay saN-pluh
– round-trip	– aller-retour ah-lay-ruh-tour
– business class	– en classe affaire ahN klahss ah-fehr

▶ *Numbers, see inside front cover*

I'd like *a window* / *an aisle seat*.	J'aimerais bien une place *côté fenêtre* / *côté couloir*. zhem-eh-reh bee-aN ewn plahss *ko-teh fuh-neh-truh* / *ko-teh kool-wahr*
Can I take this as a carry-on?	Est-ce que je peux prendre cela comme bagages à main? es-kuh zhuh puh prahN-druh suh-lah kom bah-gahzh ah maN
I'd like to … my flight.	Je voudrais … mon vol. zhuh voo-dreh … mohN vol
– confirm	– reconfirmer ruh-kohn-feer-may
– cancel	– annuler ah-newl-lay
– change	– modifier mo-dee-fyeh

Airport: Additional Words

airport	l'aéroport *m* lah-ehr-o-por
airport shuttle bus	la navette (d'aéroport) lah nah-vet (dah-ehr-o-por)
airport tax	la taxe d'aéroport lah tahx dah-ehr-o-por
arrival	l'arrivée *f* lah-ree-veh
boarding pass	la carte d'embarquement lah cahrt dahN-bahrk-mahN
check-in desk	le guichet luh gee-sheh
connecting flight	la correspondance lah kah-rehs-ohN-dahNs
delay	le retard luh ruh-tahr
departure	le départ luh day-pahr
exit	la sortie lah saw-tee
flight attendant	le steward / l'hôtesse de l'air *f* luh stew-ahr / lo-tess duh-lehr
flying time	la durée du vol lah dew-ray dew vol

41

landing	l'atterrissage *m* lah-tehr-ee-sahzh
local time	l'heure *f* locale luhr lo-kahl
pilot	le pilote luh pee-lot
plane	l'avion *m* lah-vee-ohN
return flight	le vol de retour luh vol duh ruh-tewr
sick bag	le sachet en cas de nausée
	luh sah-sheh ahN kah duh no-zeh
stopover	l'escale *f* les-kahl

Travel by Train

Information and Tickets

Where can I find the *baggage storage / lockers*?	Où est la *consigne / consigne automatique*? oo eh lah *kohN-seen-yuh / kohN-seen-yuh o-toh-mah-teek*
When's the next train to ...?	A quelle heure part le prochain train pour ...? ah kel uhr pahr luh pro-shaN traN poor
When does it arrive in ...?	A quelle heure arrive-t-il à ...? ah kel uhr ah-reev-teel ah
Do I have to change trains?	Je dois changer? zhuh dwah shahN-zheh
Which track does the train to ... leave from?	De quel quai part le train pour ...? duh kel keh pahr luh traN poor
Are there discounts for ...	Est-ce qu'il y a une réduction pour ... es-keel ya ewn ray-dewk-see-ohN poor
– families?	– les familles? lay fah-mee
– children?	– les enfants? lay-zahN-fahN
– students?	– les étudiants? lay-zeh-tew-dyahN

A ... ticket to ..., please.	Un billet ... pour ..., s'il vous plaît. aN bee-yeh ... poor ... see voo play
– one way	– aller simple ah-lay saN-pluh
– round trip	– aller retour ah-lay ruh-tour
– child fare	– pour enfants poor ahN-fahN
– adult	– pour adultes poor ah-dewlt

I'd like to reserve a seat.
Je voudrais réserver une place.
zhuh voo-dreh ray-zehr-veh ewn plahss

I'd like ...
Je voudrais ... zhuh voo-dreh

– a window seat.
– une place à côté de la fenêtre.
ewn plahss ah ko-teh duh lah fuh-neh-truh

– an aisle seat.
– une place à côté du couloir.
ewn plahss ah ko-teh dew kool-wah

– non-smoking
– non-fumeur nohN-few-muhr

– smoking
– fumeur few-muhr

I'd like to take my bicycle with me.
Je voudrais emporter mon vélo.
zhuh voo-dreh ahN-paw-teh mohN veh-lo

info Validate your ticket at the train station by inserting it in an orange machine - machine à composter or composteur. Otherwise you may get fined by the conductor.

At the Train Station

Accès aux quais	To the platforms
Consigne automatique	Lockers
Douches	Showers
Eau non potable	Non-potable water
Eau potable	Drinking water
La consigne	Baggage Storage

La sortie	Exit
Renseignements	Information
Restaurant de la gare	Station Restaurant
Salle d'attente	Waiting room
Toilettes	Restrooms
Voie	Track

On the Train

Is this the train to …?	C'est le train pour …? say luh traN poor
Is this seat taken?	Est-ce que cette place est occupée? es-kuh set plahss eh-tawk-ew-pay
Excuse me, that's my seat.	Excusez-moi, c'est ma place. ex-kew-zeh-mwah say mah plahss
Could you help me, please?	Est-ce que vous pouvez m'aider, s'il vous plaît? es-kuh voo poo-veh meh-day see voo play
Do you mind if I *open* / *close* the window?	Vous permettez que *j'ouvre* / *je ferme* la fenêtre? voo pehr-meh-teh kuh *zhoo-vruh* / *zhuh fehrm* lah fuh-neh-truh
How many more stops to …?	Combien y a-t-il encore d'arrêts jusqu'à …? kohN-bee-aN yah-teel ahN-kaw dah-reh zhews-kah
How long does the train stop here?	Combien de temps dure l'arrêt? kohN-bee-aN duh tahN dewr lah-reh
Will I catch my connection to …?	Est-ce que j'aurai le train pour …? es-kuh zhoh-ray luh traN poor

Travel by Train: Additional Words

arrival	l'arrivée f lah-ree-veh
car	la voiture lah vwah-tewr
class	la classe lah klahss
compartment	le compartiment
	luh kohN-pahr-tee-mahN
conductor	le contrôleur luh kohN-tro-luhr
connection	la correspondance
	lah koh-res-pohN-dahNs
departure	le départ luh day-pahr
dining car	le wagon-restaurant
	luh vah-gohN-res-toh-rahN
exit	la sortie lah saw-tee
fare	le prix du billet luh pree dew bee-yeh
luggage car	le wagon à bagages
	luh vah-gohN ah bah-gahzh
non-smoking	le compartiment non-fumeurs luh
compartment	kohN-pahr-tee-mahN nohN few-muhr
platform	le quai luh keh
reserved	réservé ray-zehr-veh
schedule	l'horaire m lo-rehr
seat	la place lah plahss
sleeper car	le wagon-lit luh vah-gohN-lee
smoking compartment	le compartiment fumeurs
	luh kohN-pahr-tee-mahN few-muhr
surcharge	le supplément luh sewp-pluh-mahN
to arrive	arriver ah-ree-veh
to change trains	changer de train
	shahN-zheh duh traN
to get off	descendre day-sahN-druh
to get on	monter mohN-teh
track	voie vwah
train	le train luh traN
train station	la gare lah gahr

Travel by Bus

How do I get to the bus station?	Comment est-ce que je peux faire pour aller à la gare routière? kohN-mahN es-kuh zhuh puh fehr poor ah-lay ah lah gahr roo-tyehr
When does the next bus to … leave?	Quand part le prochain car pour…? kahN pahr luh pro-shaN kahr poor
A ticket / Two tickets to …, please.	*Un ticket / Deux tickets* pour …, s'il vous plaît. *aN tee-keh / duh tee-keh* poor… see voo play
Could you tell me where I have to get off?	Pouvez-vous me dire où je dois descendre? poo-veh-voo muh deer oo zhuh dwah day-sahN-druh
How long does the trip last?	Combien de temps dure le voyage? kohN-bee-aN duh tahN dewr luh vwah-yahzh

info Tickets can normally be purchased from the bus driver, but you must always validate your ticket in the machine (composter votre billet).

Travel by Boat

Information and Reservations

| When does the next *boat / ferry* leave for …? | Quand part le prochain *bateau / ferry* pour …? kahN pahr luh pro-shaN *bah-toh / fehr-ree* poor |
| How long is the trip to …? | Combien de temps dure la traversée pour …? kohN-bee-aN duh tahn dewr lah trah-vehr-say poor |

When do we dock in …?	Quand est-ce qu'on accoste à …? kahN-tes-kohN ah-kawst ah
When do we have to be on board?	Quand devons-nous être à bord? kahN duh-vohN-noo eh-truh ah bohr
I'd like *a first* / *an economy* class boat ticket to …	Je voudrais un billet de bateau en *première classe* / *classe touriste* pour … zhuh voo-dreh aN bee-yeh duh bah-toh ahN *prem-yehr klahss* / *klahss toor-eest* poor
I'd like …	Je voudrais … zhuh voo-dreh
– a single cabin.	– une cabine individuelle. ewn kah-been aN-dee-vee-dew-el
– a twin cabin.	– une cabine à deux places. ewn kah-been ah duh plahss
– an outside cabin.	– une cabine extérieure. ewn kah-been ex-tehr-ee-uhr
– an inside cabin.	– une cabine intérieure. ewn kah-been aN-tehr-ee-uhr

Aboard

I'm looking for cabin number …	Je cherche la cabine numéro … zhuh shehrsh lah kah-been new-meh-ro
Could I have another cabin?	Est-ce que je pourrais changer de cabine? es-kuh zhuh poo-reh shaN-zheh duh kah-been
Do you have anything for seasickness?	Vous avez un remède contre le mal de mer? voo-zah-veh aN ruh-med kohN-truh luh mahl duh mehr

47

Boat Trips: Additional Words

air conditioning	la climatisation
	lah klee-mah-tee-sah-see-ohN
blanket	la couverture lah koo-vehr-tewr
captain	le capitaine luh kah-pee-ten
car ferry	le car-ferry le kahr-feh-ree
coast	la côte lah koht
cruise	la croisière lah krwah-zee-ehr
deck	le pont luh pohN
deckchair	la chaise longue lah shehz lohNg
dock	le point d'accostage
	luh pwahN dah-kaws-tahzh
land excursion	l'excursion *f* à terre
	lex-kewr-zee-ohN ah tehr
life jacket	le gilet de sauvetage
	luh gee-leh duh sohv-tahzh
life preserver	la bouée de sauvetage
	lah boo-eh duh sohv-tahzh
lifeboat	l'embarcation *f* de sauvetage lahN-
	bahr-kah-see-ohN duh sohv-tahzh
rough seas	la mer agitée lah mehr ah-zhee-teh
ship	le bateau luh bah-toh
shipping agency	l'agence *f* maritime
	lah-zhahNs mah-ree-teem
ship's doctor	le médecin de bord
	luh med-saN duh bohr
steward	le steward luh stew-ahr

Travel by Car and Motorcycle

Rental

I'd like to rent …	Je voudrais louer … zhuh voo-dreh loo-eh
– a car.	– une voiture. ewn vwah-tewr
– an automatic car.	– une voiture à embrayage automatique. ewn vwah-tewr ah ahN-bray-ahzh o-toh-mah-teek
– an off-road vehicle.	– un quatre-quatre. aN kah-truh-kah-truh
– a motorbike.	– une moto. ewn mo-toh
– an RV (recreational vehicle).	– un camping-car. aN kahN-ping-kahr
Est-ce que je pourrais voir votre permis de conduire (international)?	Could I see your (international) driver's license, please?

I'd like to rent it for …	Je voudrais la louer pour … zhuh voo-dreh lah loo-eh poor
– tomorrow.	– demain. duh-maN
– one day.	– une journée. ewn zhoor-nay
– two days.	– deux jours. duh zhoor
– a week.	– une semaine. ewn suh-men
How much does that cost?	Combien ça coûte? kohN-bee-aN sah koot
Is mileage included?	Est-ce que le kilométrage est compris? es-kuh luh kee-low-meh-trahzh eh kohN-pree
Does it include fully comprehensive insurance?	L'assurance tous risques est comprise? lah-sew-rahNs too-reesk eh kohN-pree
Can I also return the car in …?	Je peux aussi restituer la voiture à …? zhuh puh o-see res-tee-tew-eh lah vwah-tewr ah
When do I have to be back by?	A quelle heure est-ce que je dois être de retour? ah kel uhr es kuh zhuh dwah eh-truh duh ruh-toor
Please give me a crash helmet as well.	Donnez-moi aussi un casque (de protection), s'il vous plaît. dun-nay-mwah o-see aN kahsk (duh pro-tek-see-ohN) see voo play

info The minimum age for renting a car ranges from 21 to 25, depending on the rental company. Most rental firms require you to have a major credit card.

At the Gas / Petrol Station

Where's the nearest gas station?	Où se trouve la station-service la plus proche? oo suh troov lah stah-see-ohN-sehr-vees lah plew prawsh
Fill it up, please.	Le plein, s'il vous plaît. luh plaN see voo play
… euros worth of …, please.	Pour … euro …, s'il vous plaît. poor …uh-ro … see voo play
– unleaded	– d'ordinaire sans plomb daw-dee-nehr sahN plohN
– super unleaded	– de super sans plomb duh sew-pehr sahN plohN
– diesel	– de gas-oil duh gah-zol
I'd like *one liter / two liters* of oil.	Je voudrais *1 litre / 2 litres* d'huile. zhuh voo-dray *aN lee-truh / duh lee-truh* dweel

▶ *Numbers, see inside front cover*

Breakdown

I've run out of gas.	Je suis en panne sèche. zhuh sweez-ahN pahn sesh
I've got a *flat tire / engine trouble.*	J'ai *un pneu crevé / une panne de moteur.* zheh *aN pnuh kruh-veh / ewn pahn duh mo-tuhr*
Could you give me a jump-start?	Est-ce que vous pouvez m'aider à démarrer la voiture? es-kuh voo poo-veh med-eh ah day-mah-ray lah vwah-tewr

Could you …	Est-ce que vous pourriez …
	es-kuh voo poor-ee-eh
– give me a ride?	– m'emmener un bout de chemin?
	mahN-muh-neh aN boo duh shuh-maN
– tow my car?	– remorquer ma voiture?
	ruh-maw-keh mah vwah-tewr
– send me a tow truck?	– m'envoyer la dépanneuse?
	mahN-vwah-yeh lah day-pahn-nuhz

Accidents

Please call …, quick!	Vite, appelez … veet ah-play
– an ambulance	– une ambulance!
	ewn ahN-bew-lahNs
– the police	– la police! lah po-leess
– the fire station	– les pompiers! lay pohN-pyeh
There's been an accident!	Il y a eu un accident!
	eel-yah ew aN ahk-see-dahN
… people have been (seriously) hurt.	Il y a … blessés (graves).
	eel-yah … bless-eh (grahv)
I need a first-aid kit.	J'ai besoin de pansements.
	zheh buh-zwahN duh pahNs-mahN
It wasn't my fault.	Ce n'est pas de ma faute.
	suh nay pah duh mah foht
I'd like to call the police.	Je voudrais que l'on appelle la police. zhuh voo-dray kuh lohN ah-pel lah po-leess
I had right of way.	J'avais la priorité.
	zhah-veh lah pree-or-ee-teh

You were tailgating.	Vous m'avez collé. voo mah-veh kaw-lay
You were driving too fast.	Vous rouliez trop vite. vooz roo-lee-eh tro veet
Give me your name and address, please.	Donnez-moi votre nom et votre adresse, s'il vous plaît. dun-nay-mwah vo-truh nohN eh vo-truh ah-dress see voo play
Would you act as my witness?	Vous pouvez servir de témoin? voo poo-veh sehr-veer duh teh-mwahN

Getting Your Car Fixed

Where's the nearest garage?	Où est le garage le plus proche? oo eh luh gah-rahzh luh plew prawsh
The car is on the road to …	La voiture est sur la route à … lah vwah-tewr eh sewr lah root ah
Can you tow it?	Vous pouvez la remorquer? voo poo-veh lah ruh-maw-keh
Could you have a look at it?	Vous pourriez vérifier, s'il vous plaît? voo poor-ee-eh veh-ree-fee-eh see voo play
… isn't working.	… ne marche pas. nuh mahrsh pah

▶ *Car and Motorcycle: Additional Words, page 55*

My car won't start.	Ma voiture ne démarre pas. mah vwah-tewr nuh day-mahr pah
The battery's dead.	La batterie est vide. lah bah-teh-ree eh veed

The engine *sounds funny / doesn't have any power.*	Le moteur *fait un bruit bizarre / ne tire pas.* luh mo-tuhr *feh aNh brwee bee-zahr / nuh teer pah*
Can I still drive the car?	Est-ce que je peux encore rouler avec la voiture ? es-kuh zhuh puh ahN-kaw roo-lay ah-vek lah vwah-tewr
About how much will the repairs cost?	Combien va coûter la réparation, à peu près? kohN-bee-aN vah koo-teh lah ray-pah-rah-see-ohN ah puh preh
When will it be ready?	Elle sera prête quand? el suh-rah preht kahN
Do you accept coupons from the … insurance?	Vous acceptez les chèques de mon assurance multirisque …? voo zahk-sep-teh lay shek duh mohN ah-sew-rahns mewl-tee-reesk

Car and Motorcycle: Additional Words

accident insurance	le contrat multirisque de garantie automobile luh kohN-trah mewl-tee-reesk duh gah-rahN-tee oh-toh-moh-beel
accident report	le constat à l'amiable luh kohN-stah ah lah-mee-ah-bluh
air conditioning	la climatisation lah klee-mah-tee-sah-see-ohN
air filter	le filtre à air luh feel-truh ah ehr
alternator	la dynamo lah dee-nah-mo
antifreeze	l'antigel m lahN-tee-zhel
axle	l'essieu m less-yuh
battery	la batterie lah bah-tuh-ree
brake	le frein luh fraN
brake fluid	le liquide des freins luh lee-keed day fraN
brake light	le feu de stop luh fuh duh stawp
broken	cassé kah-say
bumper	le pare-chocs luh pahr-shohk
car key	la clé de la voiture lah klay duh lah vwah-tewr
car seat	le siège pour enfant luh see-ehzh poor ahN-fahN
carburetor	le carburateur luh kah-bew-rah-tuhr
catalytic converter	le pot catalytique luh poh kah-tah-lee-teek
clutch	l'embrayage m lahN-bray-ahzh
coolant	le liquide de refroidissement luh lee-keed duh ruh-fwah-deess-mahN
country road	la route départementale lah root day-paht-mahN-tahl
crash	le tamponnement luh tahN-pun-mahN

curve	le virage *m* luh vee-rahzh
to drive	conduire kohN-dweer
driver's license	le permis de conduire
	luh pehr-mee-duh kohN-dweer
emergency brake	le frein à main luh fraN ah maN
emergency triangle	le triangle de signalisation luh tree-
	ahN-gluh duh seen-yahl-ee-sah-see-
	ohN
engine	le moteur luh moh-tuhr
engine oil	l'huile *f* moteur lweel moh-tuhr
exhaust	le pot d'échappement
	luh poh day-shahp-mahN
expressway	l'autoroute *f* lo-toh-root
fanbelt	la courroie lah koor-wah
fender	l'aile *f* leh-luh
finish	la laque lah lahk
fire extinguisher	l'extincteur *m* lex-taNk-tuhr
first-aid kit	la boîte de premiers secours
	lah bwaht duh pruh-mee-eh suh-koor
fuse	le fusible luh few-zee-bluh
garage	le garage luh gah-rahzh
gas canister	le jerricane luh zheh-ree-kahn
gas station	la station-service
	lah stah-see-ohN-sehr-veess
gasket	le joint luh zhwaN
gear	la vitesse lah vee-tess
green insurance card	la carte verte lah kaht vehrt
headlights	le phare luh fah
heat	le chauffage luh show-fahzh
helmet	le casque luh kahsk
hood	le capot luh kah-poh
horn	le klaxon luh klahx-ohN
ignition	l'allumage *m* lah-lew-mahzh
ignition cable	le fil d'allumage
	luh feel dah-lew-mahzh

jumper cables	les câbles de démarrage
	lay kah-bluh duh day-mah-rahzh
kilometer	le kilomètre luh kee-low-meh-truh
light	le feu luh fuh
light bulb	l'ampoule *f* lahN-pool
luggage rack	le porte-bagages
	luh pawt-bah-gahzh
mirror	le miroir luh meer-wahr
motorbike	la moto lah moh-toh
multi-level parking garage	le parking couvert
	luh pah-king koo-vehr
neutral	le point mort luh pwaN maw
no-parking zone	l'interdiction *f* de stationner
	laN-tehr-deek-see-ohN duh stah-see-
	ohN-nay
oil change	la vidange lah vee-dahNzh
to park	se garer suh gah-ray
parking disc	le disque horaire luh deesk oh-rehr
parking lot	le parking luh pah-king
parking meter	le parcmètre luh pahk-meh-truh
radiator	le radiateur luh rah-dee-ah-tuhr
ramp	la voie d'accès à l'autoroute
	lah vwah dahk-say ah lo-toh-root
rear-end collision	le télescopage
	luh teh-leh-skoh-pahzh
rear-view mirror	le rétroviseur luh ray-tro-vee-suhr
repair	la réparation
	lah ray-pah-rah-see-ohN
to repair	réparer ray-pah-ray
to replace	changer shahN-zheh
right of way	la priorité lah pree-aw-ree-teh
RV (recreational vehicle)	le camping-car luh kahN-ping-kah
seatbelt	la ceinture de sécurité
	lah saN-tewr duh say-kew-ree-teh
service area	le relais routier luh ruh-lay roo-tyeh

shock absorber	l'amortisseur *m* lah-maw-tees-suhr
snow chains	les chaînes *f/pl* à neige
	lay shehn ah nehzh
spare tire	la roue de secours
	lah roo duh suh-koor
spark plug	la bougie lah boo-zhee
speedometer	le compteur de vitesse
	luh kohN-tuhr duh vee-tess
starter	le démarreur luh day-mah-ruhr
steering	la direction lah dee-rek-see-ohN
sunroof	le toit ouvrant luh twah oov-rahN
switch	le guichet luh ghee-sheh
tail light	les feux *m/pl* arrière
	lay fuh ah-ree-ehr
tire	le pneu luh pnuh
tire pressure	la pression des pneus
	lah pres-see-ohN day pnuh
toll	le péage luh pay-ahzh
tow rope	le câble de remorquage
	luh kah-bluh duh ruh-maw-kahzh
tow truck	la dépanneuse lah day-pahn-nuhz
transmission	la boîte de vitesses
	lah bwaht duh vee-tess
valve	la valve lah vahlv
vehicle registration	la carte grise lah kaht greez
wheel	la roue lah roo
windshield wipers	l'essuie-glace *m* less-wee glahss
wiper blades	les balais *m/pl* d'essuie-glace
	lay bah-lay dess-wee-glahss
witness	le témoin luh teh-mwahN

Public Transportation

info Subway fares are standard regardless of the distance you travel. Tickets are less expensive if you buy a book of ten (un carnet). The Paris metro closes from 12:50 am to 5:30 am.

Where's the nearest subway station?	Où est la station de métro la plus proche? oo eh lah stah-asee-ohN duh may-troh lah plew prawsh
Where's the nearest bus stop?	Où est l'arrêt d'autobus le plus proche? oo eh lah-ray-doto-bewss luh plew prawsh
Where is the bus stop to …?	Où est l'arrêt d'autobus pour…? oo eh lah-ray doh-toh-bewss poor
Which *bus / subway* goes to …?	*Quel bus / Quel métro* va à …? *kel bewss / kel may-tro* vah ah

METROPOLITAIN

Le bus numéro …	The bus number …
La ligne …	The … line.
When's the next *bus / subway* to …?	A quelle heure part le prochain *autobus / métro* pour …? ah kel uhr pahr luh pro-shaN *oh-toh-bewws / may-tro* poor
Does this bus go to …?	Est-ce que ce bus va à …? es-kuh suh bewss vah ah
Do I have to transfer to get to …?	Pour …, est-ce que je dois changer? poor … es-kuh zhuh dwah shahN-zheh
Could you tell me where I have to *get off / transfer*?	Pouvez-vous me dire où je dois *descendre / changer*? poo-veh voo muh deer oo zhuh dwah *day-sahN-druh / shahN-zheh*
A ticket to …, please.	Un ticket pour …, s'il vous plaît. aN tee-keh poor … see voo play
Do you have …	Il y a … eel yah
– a one day travel pass?	– des tickets pour la journée? day tee-keh poor lah zhoor-nay
– multiple-ride tickets?	– des carnets? day kah-nay
– weekly travel passes?	– des cartes hebdomadaires? day kahrt eb-doh-mah-dehr
– a booklet of tickets?	– un carnet de tickets? aN kah-nay duh tee-keh

Numbers, see inside front cover

Taking a Taxi

Could you call a taxi for me (for tomorrow morning) for … o'clock?	Vous pourriez m'appeler un taxi pour (demain à) … heures ? voo poor-ee-eh mah-play aN tahx-ee poor (duh-maN ah) … uhr
…, please.	…, s'il vous plaît. see voo play
– To the train station	– A la gare ah lah gah
– To the airport	– A l'aéroport ah lah-eh-roh-paw
– To the … Hotel	– A l'hôtel … ah loh-tel
– To the city center	– Au centre ville oh sahN-truh veel
– To … Street	– Rue … rew
How much is it to …?	Combien ce sera pour aller à …? kohN-bee-aN suh suh-rah poor ah-lay ah
Please *turn on / reset* the meter.	Mettez votre compteur *en marche / sur zéro*, s'il vous plaît. meh-teh vo-truh kohN-tuhr *ahN mahsh / sewr zeh-ro* see voo play
Please *wait / stop* here (for a moment).	*Attendez / Arrêtez-vous* (un instant) ici, s'il vous plaît. *ah-tahN-day / ah-ret-teh voo* (aN aN-stahN) ee-see see voo play
Keep the change.	Gardez la monnaie. gah-day lah mun-eh

Public Transportation and Taxi: Additional Words

bus station	la gare routière lah gah roo-tee-ehr
bus stop	l'arrêt *m* de bus lah-ray duh bewss
city center	le centre-ville luh sahN-truh veel
conductor	le contrôleur luh kohN-traw-luhr

61

departure	le départ luh day-pah
direction	la direction lah dee-rek-see-ohN
driver	le chauffeur luh shoh-fuhr
fare	le prix du billet luh pree dew bee-yeh
to get off	descendre day-sahN-druh
last stop	le terminus luh tehr-mee-newss
local train	le RER luh ehr-uh-ehr
schedule	l'horaire *m* loh-rehr
stop	l'arrêt *m* lah-ray
to stop	s'arrêter sah-ray-tay
taxi stand	la station de taxis lah stah-see-ohN duh tahx-ee
ticket	le ticket luh tee-keh
ticket machine	le distributeur automatique de tickets luh deess-tree-bew-tuhr oh-toh-mah-teek duh tee-keh
ticket validation machine	le composteur luh kohN-paws-tuhr
to transfer (train)	changer de train shahN-zheh duh traN
to validate	composter kohN-paws-teh

Travel
with
Children

How old is your child?
Votre enfant a quel âge?

Do you have a children's menu?
Avez-vous un menu enfant?

Frequently Asked Questions

Is there a children's discount?	Vous faites une réduction pour les enfants? voo feht ewn ray-dewk-see-ohN poor lay-zahN-fahN
How old do they have to be?	*Jusqu'à / A partir de* quel âge? *zhews-kah / ah pahr-teer duh* kel ahzh
Tickets for two adults and two children, please.	Des billets pour deux adultes et deux enfants, s'il vous plaît. day bee-yeh poor duh-zah-dewlt eh duh-zahN-fahN see voo play
Is there a children's playground here?	Il y a un terrain de jeu pour enfants ici? eel-yah aN tehr-aN duh zhuh poor ahN-fahN ee-see
How old is your child?	Votre enfant a quel âge? vo-truh ahN-fahN ah kel ahzh
My daughter / My son is ….	*Ma fille / Mon fils* a … ans. *mah fee / mohN feess* ah … ahN

Where can we buy …	Où peut-on acheter … oo puh-tohN ahsh-teh
– baby food?	– l'alimentation pour bébés? lah-lee-mahN-tah-see-ohN poor bay-bay
– children's clothes?	– les vêtements pour enfants? lay vet-mahN poor ahN-fahN
– diapers?	– les couches? lay koosh
Do you have special offers for children?	Avez-vous des promotions spéciales pour les enfants? ah-veh-voo day promo-see-ohN speh-see-ahl poor lay-zahN-fahN
Have you seen a little *girl / boy*?	Avez-vous vu *une petite fille / un petit garçon*? ah-veh-voo vew *ewn puh-teet fee / aN puh-tee gahr-sohN*
Is there a children's section?	Il y a un compartiment pour enfants? eel-yah aN kohN-pahr-tee-mahN poor ahN-fahN
Do you have a car seat for the rental car?	Avez-vous aussi un siège pour enfants dans la voiture de location? ah-veh-voo o-see aN see-ehz poor ahN-fahN dahN lah vwah-tewr duh loh-kah-see-ohN
Can I rent a child seat for a bicycle?	Je peux louer un siège à vélo pour enfants? zhuh puh loo-eh aN see-ehz ah veh-lo poor ahN-fahN
Up to what age can children travel free?	Jusqu'à quel âge le trajet est gratuit pour les enfants? zhews-kah kel ahzh luh trah-zheh eh grah-twee poor lay-zahN-fahN

At the Hotel / Restaurant

Could you put in a cot?	Pourriez-vous installer un lit d'enfant? poo-ree-eh-voo aN-stah-lay aN lee dahN-fahN
Is there day care?	Peut-on faire garder les enfants? puh-tohN fehr gahr-day lay-zahN-fahN
Do you have a high chair?	Avez-vous une chaise haute pour enfants? ah-veh-voo ewn shehz oht poor ahN-fahN
Could you please warm the bottle?	Pourriez-vous réchauffer le biberon, s'il vous plaît? poor-ee-eh-voo ray-shoh-feh luh bee-buh-rohN see voo play
Do you have a children's menu?	Avez-vous un menu enfant? ah-veh voo aN muh-new ahN-fahN
Could we get half portions for the children?	Est-ce qu'on peut avoir des demies portions pour les enfants? es-kohN puh ah-vwahr day duh-mee por-see-ohN poor lay-zahN-fahN
Could we please have another place setting?	Pourrions-nous avoir un autre couvert, s'il vous plaît? poor-ee-ohN noo-zah-vwah aN o-truh koo-vehr see voo play

Swimming with Children

Is it dangerous for children?	C'est dangereux pour les enfants? say dahN-zheh-ruh poor lay-zahN-fahN

66

| Is there a children's pool as well? | Il y a aussi un bassin pour enfants? eel-yah o-see aN bah-saN poor ahN-fahN |
| How deep is the water? | Quelle est la profondeur de l'eau? kel eh lah pro-fohN-duhr duh loh |

Childcare and Health

| Can you recommend a reliable babysitter? | Pouvez-vous nous recommander une babysitter sérieuse? poo-veh-voo noo ruh-kohN-mahN-day ewn beh-bee-sit-tehr sehr-ee-uhz |
| My child is allergic to milk products. | Mon enfant est allergique aux produits laitiers. mohN-nahN-fahN eh ahl-lehr-zheek oh pro-dwee lay-tyeh |

► *Health, page 175*

Travel with Children: Additional Words

allergy	l'allergie *f* lah-lehr-zhee
baby bottle	le biberon luh bee-buh-rohN
baby phone / monitor	l'interphone *m* de surveillance pour bébés laN-tehr-fohn duh sewr-veh-yahNss poor bay-bay
baby powder	le talc luh tahlk
bottle warmer	le chauffe-biberon luh chohf-bee-buh-rohN
boy	le garçon luh gahr-sohN
child safety belt	la ceinture de sécurité pour enfants lah sahN-tewr duh say-kew-ree-teh poor ahN-fahN

children's portion	l'assiette *f* pour enfants
	lah-see-eht poor ahN-fahN
children's supplement	le supplément pour enfants
	luh sew-pluh-mahN poor ahN-fahN
coloring book	le livre de coloriage
	luh leev-ruh duh koh-lohr-ee-ahzh
cot	le lit d'enfant luh lee dahN-fahN
crayon	le crayon de pastel
	luh kray-ohN de pahss-tel
daughter	la fille lah fee
girl	la petite fille lah puh-teet fee
insect bite	la piqûre d'insecte
	lah pee-kewr dahN-sect
mosquito repellent	la protection contre les moustiques
	lah pro-tek-see-ohN kohN-truh lay
	moo-steek
nipple	la tétine lah teh-teen
pacifier	la sucette lah sew-set
picture book	le livre d'images pour enfants luh
	lee-vruh dee-mahzh poor ahN-fahN
playground	le terrain de jeux
	luh tehr-aN duh zhuh
playpen	le parc luh pahrk
rash	l'eczéma *m* leg-zem-ah
son	le fils luh feess
stroller	la poussette lah poo-set
toy	le jouet luh zhoo-eh
vaccination card	le carnet de vaccinations luh kahr-
	nay duh vahk-see-nah-see-ohN
visored cap	la casquette à visière
	lah kahs-ket ah vee-zee-ehr

For the Disabled

Could you open the door for me?
Vous pourriez m'ouvrir la porte?

Do you have a wheelchair I could use?
Avez-vous un fauteuil roulant pour moi?

Asking for Help

Could you help me, please?	Pouvez-vous m'aider, s'il vous plaît? poo-veh-voo med-eh see voo play
I have mobility problems.	Je suis une personne à mobilité réduite. zhuh swee ewn pehr-sun ah mo-bee-lee-teh ray-dweet
I'm disabled.	Je suis handicapé physique. zhuh swee ahn-dee-kah-pay fee-zeek
I'm visually impaired.	Je suis ♂ malvoyant / ♀ malvoyante. zhuh swee ♂ mahl-vwah-yahN / ♀ mahl-vwah-yahNt
I'm *hearing impaired* / *deaf*.	Je suis ♂ *malentendant* / ♀ *malentendante* / ♂ *sourd* / ♀ *sourde*. zhuh swee ♂ *mahl-ahN-tahn-dahN* / ♀ *mahl-ahN-tahn-dahNt* / ♂ *soor* / ♀ *soord*
I'm hard of hearing.	Je n'entends pas bien. zhuh nahN-tahn pah bee-aN
Could you speak up a bit, please?	Vous pourriez parler plus fort, s'il vous plaît? voo-poor-ee-eh pahr-lay plew for see voo play
Could you write that down?	Vous pouvez me l'écrire? voo poo-veh muh lay-creer
Is it suitable for wheelchair users?	Est-ce que c'est aménagé pour re-cevoir les handicapés en fauteuil roulant? es kuh say ah-men-ah-zheh poor ruh-suh-vwah lay ahN-dee-kah-pay ahN fo-tuh-yuh roo-lahN

Is there a wheelchair ramp?	Il y a une rampe pour les fauteuils roulants? eel-yah ewn rahNp poor lay fo-tuh-yuh roo-lahN
Is there a wheelchair-accessible restroom here?	Il y a des toilettes pour handicapés ici? eel-yah day twah-let poor ahN-dee-kah-pay ee-see
Can I bring my (collapsible) wheelchair?	Est-ce que je peux emmener mon fauteuil roulant (pliable)? es kuh zhuh puh ahNm-nay mohN fo-tuh-yuh roo-lahN (plee-ah-bluh)
Could you please help me get *on / off*?	Vous pourriez m'aider *à descendre / à sortir*, s'il vous plaît? voo poor-ee-eh meh-day *ah day-sahN-druh / ah saw-teer* see voo play
Could you *open / hold open* the door for me?	Vous pourriez *m'ouvrir la porte / me tenir la porte ouverte.* voo poor-ee-eh *moov-reer lah pawrt / muh tuh-neer lah pawrt oo-vehrt*
Do you have a seat where I can stretch my legs?	Avez-vous une place où je pourrais allonger les jambes? ah-veh-voo ewn plahss oo zhuh poor-eh ah-lohN-zheh lay zhahNb

At the Hotel

Does the hotel have facilities for the disabled?	L'hôtel est équipé pour recevoir les handicapés? loh-tel eh eh-kee-pay poor ruh-suh-vwah lay ahN-dee-kah-pay
Does it have a ramp for wheelchairs?	Il y a une rampe pour les fauteuils roulants? eel-yah ewn rahNp poor lay fo-tuh-yuh roo-lahN

Do you have a wheelchair I could use?	Avez-vous un fauteuil roulant pour moi? ah-veh voo aN fo-tuh-yuh roo-lahN poor mwah
Could you take my luggage *up to my room* / *to the taxi*?	Pouvez-vous transporter mes bagages *dans ma chambre* / *jusqu'au taxi*? poo-veh-voo trahN-spawr-teh may bah-gahzh *dahN mah shahN-bruh* / *zhews-ko tahx-ee*
Where's the nearest elevator?	Où est l'ascenseur le plus proche? oo eh lah-sahN-suhr luh plew prawsh
Could you call for me?	Pouvez-vous me composer le numéro? poo-veh-voo muh kohN-paw-say luh new-may-ro

For the Disabled: Additional Words

companion	l'accompagnateur *m* / l'accompagnatrice *f* lah-kohN-pahn-yah-tuhr / lah-kohN-pahn-yah-treess
crutch	la béquille lah bay-kee-yuh
guide dog	le chien d'aveugle luh shee-aN dah-vuh-gluh
level access	au niveau du sol oh-nee-voh dew sol
mobility cane	la canne pour nonvoyants lah kahn poor nohN-vwah-yahN
paraplegic	paraplégique pah-rah-play-zheek
suitable for the disabled	(aménagé) pour les handicapés (ah-men-ah-zheh) poor lay ahN-dee-kah-pay
wheelchair lift	la plate-forme élévatrice lah plaht-fawrm eh-lay-vah-treess
without steps	sans marches sahN mahrsh

Communications

Where can I make a phone call?
Où est-ce que je peux téléphoner?

Where's an Internet café around here?
Où y a-t-il un cybercafé ici?

Telephone

info Purchase a télécarte at the post office (La Poste), since most public phones accept only telephone cards.

▶ *Numbers, see inside front cover*

Where can I make a phone call?	Où est-ce que je peux téléphoner? oo es kuh zhuh puh teh-lay-fohn-eh
A (… euro) phonecard, please.	Une carte téléphonique (à … euro), s'il vous plaît. ewn kahrt teh-lay-fohn-eek (ah … uh-ro) see voo play
Excuse me, I need some change for the phone.	Excusez-moi, il me faudrait des pièces pour téléphoner. ex-kew-seh mwah eel muh fo-dreh day pee-ess poor teh-lay-fohn-eh
What's the area code for …?	Quel est l'indicatif de …? kel eh laN-dee-kah-teef duh
Hello? This is ….	Allô? Je suis … ah-loh zhuh swee
I'd like to speak to …	Je voudrais parler à … zhuh voo-dreh pahr-leh ah
À l'appareil.	Speaking.
Ne quittez pas.	I'll put you through.
… est en ligne en ce moment.	… is on the other line.
… n'est malheureusement pas là.	I'm afraid … isn't here.

… n'est pas là aujourd'hui. … isn't in today.

Restez en ligne, s'il vous plaît. Hold on, please.

Pourrais-je transmettre quelque chose? Can I take a message?

What time does the evening rate start? Le tarif de nuit est valable à partir de quelle heure? luh tah-reef duh nwee eh vah-lah-bluh ah pahr-teer duh kel uhr

How much is a 3-minute call to the US? Combien coûte un appel téléphonique de trois minutes aux États-Unis? kohN-bee-aN koot aN-ah-pel teh-lay-fohn-eek duh trwah meen-ewt ohz-eh-tahs-ewn-ee

A long-distance call to …, please. Un appel longue distance pour … s'il vous plaît. aN ah-pel lohNg dees-tahNs poor … see voo play

A collect call to …, please. Un appel en PCV pour … s'il vous plaît. aN-ah-el ahN pay-say-vay poor … see voo play

Prenez la cabine … Please go to booth number …

La ligne est occupée. The line's busy.

Ça ne répond pas. There's no reply.

Internet

Where's an internet café around here?	Où y a-t-il un cybercafé ici? oo ee ah-teel aN see-behr-kah-feh ee-see
I'd like to send an e-mail.	Je voudrais envoyer un courriel. zhuh voo-dreh ahN-vwah-yeh aN koor-ee-el
Which computer can I use?	Quel ordinateur est-ce que je peux utiliser? kel aw-deen-ah-tuhr es-kuh zhuh puh ew-tee-lee-zeh
How much is it for 15 minutes?	Combien coûte quinze minutes? kohN-bee-aN koot kaNz meen-ewt
Could you help me, please?	Pourriez-vous m'aider? poor-ee-eh-voo med-eh

E-mail

annuler	Logout
boîte *f* de réception	Inbox
brouillons *m/pl*	Draft
composer	Compose
corbeille *f*	Trash
envoyer	Send
imprimer	Print
messages *m/pl* en-voyés	Outbox / Sent mail
répondre	Reply
répondre à tous	Reply all
retour	Back
sauvegarder	Save
supprimer	Delete
transférer	Forward

Eating and Drinking

The menu, please.
La carte, s'il vous plaît.

The bill, please.
L'addition, s'il vous plaît.

Reservations

Is there ... around here?	Où y a-t-il ici ... oo ee ah-teel ee-see
– a café	– un salon de thé? aN sah-lohN duh teh
– a bar	– un bistrot? aN bees-troh
– a reasonably priced restaurant	– un restaurant pas trop cher? aN rest-o-rahN pah tro shehr
A table for ..., please.	Une table pour ... personnes, s'il vous plaît. ewn tah-bluh poor ... pehr-sun see voo play
I'd like to reserve a table for *two* / *six* people for ... o'clock.	Je voudrais réserver une table pour *deux* / *six* personnes pour ... heures. zhuh voo-dreh ray-zehr-veh ewn tah-bluh poor *duh* / *seess* pehr-sohn poor ... uhr
We've reserved a table for ... people (in the name of ...)	Nous avons réservé une table pour ... personnes (au nom de ...). noo-zah-vohN ray-zehr-veh ewn tab-luh poor ... pehr-sun (oh nohN duh)
Is this *table* / *seat* free?	Est-ce que cette *table* / *place* est libre? es kuh set *tah-bluh* / *plahss* eh lee-bruh
Excuse me, where are the restrooms?	Pardon, où sont les toilettes? pahr-dohN oo sohN lay twah-let
En zone fumeurs ou non-fumeurs?	Smoking or non-smoking (area)?

info Places where you can eat: Auberge – An inn, often in the country; serves full meals and drinks. Bistrot – Selling mostly drinks and basic food (sandwiches, salads, snacks) with traditional French cuisine; usually not very expensive. Brasserie – A large café serving good, simple food and drinks, very often offering a plat du jour (dish of the day). Buffet – A restaurant found in large train stations; the food is generally good. Café / Bar – Serves coffee and drinks, sometimes light meals, too. Crêperie – Offers snacks of light pancakes with various fillings. Restaurant – Rated by scores of professional and amateur gourmets. Restoroute – A large restaurant just off a highway (motorway); table or cafeteria service is available. Rôtisserie – Specializes in meat products: roast chickens, quiches, sausages, ham, hors-d'œuvre, etc. Routier – Roughly equivalent to a roadside diner; the food is simple but can be surprisingly good.

Menu

LE MENU DU PETIT DÉJEUNER

Breakfast Menu

café *m* kah-feh — coffee
café *m* au lait kah-feh oh lay — coffee with milk
café *m* crème kah-feh krem — coffee with foamed milk
chocolat *m* chaud sho-ko-lah sho — hot chocolate
croissant *m* krwah-sahN — croissant
œuf *m*, œufs *pl* uhf uhf — egg / eggs
œuf *m* brouillé uhf broo-yeh — scrambled eggs
œuf *m* dur uhf dewr — hard-boiled egg
œuf *m* à la coque uhf ah lah kawk — soft boiled egg
thé *m* teh — tea
thé *m* au citron teh oh see-trohN — tea with lemon

MENU

POTAGES ET SOUPES

Soups

bouillabaisse *f* boo-yah-bess — fish soup from southern France
consommé *m* kohN-so-may — clear broth
soupe *f* à l'oignon gratinée soup ah lohN-yohN grah-tee-nay — onion soup, oven-browned with croutons and cheese
soupe *f* de poisson soup duh pwah-sohN — fish soup

80

HORS-D'ŒUVRE

Cold Appetizers

aspic *m* d'anguille ah-speek dahN-gwee-yuh	jellied eel
avocat *m* vinaigrette ah-vo-kah veen-eh-gret	avocado in vinaigrette sauce
charcuterie *f* shahr-kew-tree	cold cut platter
cœurs *m/pl* d'artichauts kuhr dahr-tee-sho	artichoke hearts
crevettes *f/pl* kruh-vet	shrimp
crudités *f/pl* (variées) krew-dee-teh (vah-ree-eh)	dish of raw vegetables and fruit
foie *m* gras fwah-grah	pâté de foie gras
huîtres *f/pl* we-truh	oysters
jambon *m* blanc zhahN-bohN blahN	cooked ham
jambon *m* cru zhaN-bohN krew	uncooked ham
jambon *m* fumé zhaN-bohN few-may	smoked ham
melon *m* muh lohN	melon
pâté *m* pah-teh	pâté or meat pie
pâté *m* de foie gras en croûte pah-teh duh fwah grah ahN croot	pâté de foie gras wrapped in dough
pâté *m* de foie haché fin pah-teh duh fwah ah-sheh faN	liverwurst pâté
pissenlits *m/pl* au lard pee-sahN-lee oh-lahr	dandelion salad with bacon
quiche *f* lorraine keesh law-ren	quiche with egg, cheese, and bacon

rillettes *f/pl* ree-yet	potted, finely chopped pork
salade *f* de concombres	cucumber salad
sah-lahd duh kohN-kohN-bruh	
salade *f* de tomates	tomato salad
sah-lahd duh toh-maht	
salade *f* mixte	mixed salad
sah-lahd meext	
salade *f* niçoise	green salad with
sah-lahd nee-swahz	tomatoes, eggs, anchovies and olives
saucisson *m* de campagne	liverwurst
so-see-sohN duh kahN-pahn-yuh	
saumon *m* fumé	smoked salmon
so-mohN few-may	
terrine *f* de canard	pâté / meat pie made of
teh-reen duh kah-nahr	roast duck
terrine *f* du chef	pâté / home made meat
teh-reen duh shef	pie

ENTRÉES

Hot Appetizers / Snacks

croque-monsieur *m*	toasted ham and cheese
krawk-muh-syuhr	
crêpes *f/pl* krehp	very thin pancakes
escargots *m/pl* es-kahr-go	snails
omelette *f* awm-let	omelette
omelette *f* au lard	omelette with bacon
awm-let oh lahr	
omelette *f* aux champignons	omelette with mushrooms
awm-let oh sham-peen-yohN	
omelette *f* nature	plain omelette
awm-let nah-tewr	

VIANDES

Meat Dishes

agneau *m* ahn-yo	lamb
andouillette *f* ahN-doo-yet	fried sausage made of tripe
bifteck *m* beef-tek	steak
bœuf *m* bourguignon buhf boor-geen-yohN	beef stew in red wine
bœuf *m* mode buhf mode	pot roast
bœuf *m* buhf	beef
boudin *m* noir boo-daN nwahr	blood sausage
cassoulet *m* kahss-oo-leh	beef, sausage and bean stew
côte *f* kawt	pork chops
escalope *f* panée es-kah-lawp pah-nay	breaded veal
filet *m* de bœuf fee-lay duh buhf	fillet of beef
gigot *m* d'agneau zhee-go dahn-yo	leg of lamb
grillade *f* gree-yahd	mixed grill
jarret *m* de veau zhah-reh duh vo	knuckle of veal
lièvre *m* lee-eh-vruh	wild hare
mouton *m* moo-tohN	mutton
paupiette *f* (de veau) po-pyet duh vo	slices of rolled and braised veal
pieds *m/pl* de cochon pee-yeh duh ko-shohN	pig's feet
quenelles *f/pl* kuh-nel	dumplings made from either meat or fish

ris *m* de veau ree duh vo	sweetbread
rôti *m* ro-tee	roast
sauté *m* de veau	ragout made of veal
so-teh duh vo	
selle *f* d'agneau	saddle of lamb
sell dahn-yo	
steak *m* au poivre	pepper steak
steak oh pwahv-ruh	
steak *m* haché	meat loaf
steak ahsh-eh	
tournedos *m* toor-nuh-doh	fillet steak
veau *m* vo	veal

GIBIER

Game

cerf *m* sehr	venison
civet *m* de marcassin	young wild boar in wine
see-veh duh mahr-kah-saN	sauce
médaillons *m/pl* de	medallions of venison
chevreuil	
may-dah-yohN duh shev-ruh-yuh	
sanglier *m* sahN-glee-eh	wild boar

VOLAILLE

Poultry

blanc *m* de poulet	chicken breast
blahN duh poo-leh	
canard *m* à l'orange	duck braised with
kah-nahr ah law-rahNzh	oranges and orange
	liqueur

confit *m* de canard
kohN-fee duh kah-nahr

pieces of duck, potted in its own fat

coq *m* au vin   kawk oh vaN

chicken in red or white wine sauce

pintade *f* paN-tahd

guinea fowl

poulet *m* rôti   poo-lay ro-tee

broiled chicken

POISSONS

Fish

anguille *f* ahN-gwee-yuh

eel

brandade *f* brahN-dahd

dried cod, mashed and cooked, prepared with cream, olive oil and garlic

brochet *m* braw-sheh

pike

cabillaud *m* kah-bee-yoh

cod

calmars *m/pl* frits
kahl-mahr free

fried squid rings

carpe *f* kahrp

carp

colin *m* ko-laN

hake (salt water fish, similar to a codfish)

églefin *m* ehg-luh-faN

haddock

friture *f* free-tewr

fried fish

hareng *m* saur   ahr-ahN sor

bloater, smoked herring

lotte *f* lawt

monkfish

morue *f* maw-rew

dried cod

rouget *m* roo-zheh

barbel (salt water fish with firm and lean meat)

saumon *m* so-mohN

salmon

sole *f* sawl

sole

thon *m* tohN

tuna

truite *f* trweet

trout

truite f au bleu
trweet oh bluh

poached trout

truite f aux amandes et au
beurre noir trweet oh-zah-
mahNd eh oh buhr nwahr

trout with almonds and
browned butter

truite f meunière
trweet muhn-yehr

trout turned in flour and
fried

turbot m tew-boh

turbot

Coquillages et crustacés

Seafood

coquilles f/pl Saint-Jacques
ko-kee saN-zhahk

scallops

crabe m krahb

crab

crevette f kruh-vet

shrimp, prawn

écrevisses f/pl eh-kruh-veess

fresh water crabs

homard m à l'armoricaine
oh-mahr ah lahr-mor-ee-ken

lobster in white wine
sauce

huîtres f/pl wee-truh

oysters

langouste f lahN-goost

rock lobster

langoustines f/pl
lahN-goos-teen

scampi

moules f/pl frites mool freet

mussels with French fries

plateau m de fruits de mer
plah-toh duh frwee duh mehr

seafood platter

Garnitures

Side Dishes

pâtes f/pl paht

noodles

pommes f/pl de terre
pum duh tehr

potatoes

pommes *f/pl* de terre
sautées   pum duh tehr so-teh   home fries

pommes *f/pl* de terre
vapeur   pum duh tehr vah-
puhr   boiled potatoes

pommes *f/pl* frites
pum freet   French fries

riz *m*   ree   rice

LÉGUMES

Vegetables and Legumes

artichauts *m/pl*   ahr-tee-sho   artichokes
asperges *f/pl*   ahs-pehrzh   asparagus
aubergines *f/pl*   eggplants
o-behr-zheen
carottes *f/pl*   kah-rawt   carrots
champignons *m/pl*   mushrooms
shahN-peen-yohN
champignons *m/pl* de Paris   button mushrooms
shaN-peen-yohN duh pah-ree
chou *m* fleur   shoo fluhr   cauliflower
chou *m* rave   shoo rahv   cabbage with large
                                         fleshy edible stem

chou *m* rouge   shoo roozh   red cabbage
choucroute *f*   shoo-croot   sauerkraut
choux *m/pl* de Bruxelles   Brussels sprouts
shoo duh brewx-el
courgettes *f/pl*   koor-zhet   zucchini
endives *f/pl*   ahN-deev   endives
épinards *m/pl*   eh-pee-nahr   spinach
fenouil *m*   fuh-noo-yuh   fennel

gratin m dauphinois	oven-browned potatoes
grah-taN doh-feen-wah	
haricots m/pl blancs	white beans
ah-ree-koh blahN	
haricots m/pl verts	green beans
ah-ree-koh vehr	
macédoine f de légumes	mixed vegetables
mah-seh-dwahn duh lay-gewm	
navets m/pl nah-veh	turnips
petits pois m/pl	peas
puh-tee pwah	
poivron m pwah-vrohN	bell peppers
ratatouille f rah-tah-too-yuh	vegetable dish with tomatoes, peppers, eggplant etc.

LE MODE DE PRÉPARATION

Ways of Cooking

à la broche ah lah brawsh	spit-roasted, on a skewer
(cuit) à la vapeur	steamed
(kwee) ah lah vah-puhr	
à l'étuvé ah lay-tew-veh	steamed
bien cuit bee-aN kwee	well-done
cuit au four kwee oh foor	baked
cuit à l'eau kwee ah lo	boiled
flambé flahN-bay	flambé
fumé few-may	smoked
gratiné grah-tee-nay	oven-browned
grillé gree-eh	grilled
(fait) maison (feh) may-zohN	homemade

88

| pané pah-nay | breaded |
| rôti ro-tee | roasted |

FROMAGES

Cheese

bleu *m* bluh	blue cheese
doux doo	mild
fromage *m* fro-mahzh	cheese
fromage *m* au lait cru	raw-milk cheese
fro-mahzh oh lay crew	
fromage *m* de brebis	feta cheese
fro-mahzh duh breh-bee	
fromage *m* de chèvre	goat cheese
fro-mahzh duh chehv-ruh	
plateau *m* de fromages	cheese platter
plah-toh duh fro-mahzh	

DESSERTS

Desserts

beignets *m/pl* aux pommes	apple fritters
ben-yeh oh pum	
charlotte *f* shahr-lawt	charlotte (made from vanilla cream and ladyfingers soaked in liqueur)
clafoutis *m* aux cerises	dessert made with
clahfoo-tee oh suh-reez	cherries and batter
coupe *f* maison	sundae (of the house)
koop may-zohN	

crème *f* caramel — crème caramel
krem kah-rah-mel

flan *m* flahN — flan

glace *f* glahss — ice cream

glace *f* au chocolat — chocolate ice cream
glahss oh sho-ko-lah

glace *f* à la fraise — strawberry ice cream
glahss ah lah frehz

glace *f* à la vanille — vanilla ice cream
glahss ah lah vah-nee-yuh

île *f* flottante eel floh-tahNt — merengue in custard

macédoine *f* de fruits — fruit salad
mah-seh-dwahn duh frwee

meringue *f* mehr-aNg — merengue

parfait *m* pahr-feh — parfait, soft ice cream

FRUITS

Fruit

dattes *f/pl* daht — dates

figues *f/pl* feeg — figs

fraises *f/pl* frehz — strawberries

framboises *f/pl* — raspberries
frahN-bwahz

pastèque *f* pahs-tek — watermelon

pêche *f* pehsh — peach

poire *f* pwahr — pear

pomme *f* pum — apple

raisin *m* ray-saN — grapes

GÂTEAUX ET PÂTISSERIES

Sweets and Pastries

baba *m* au rhum	yeast cake soaked in rum
bah-bah oh rohm	
chausson *m* aux pommes	apple turnover
shos-sohN oh pohm	
chou *m* à la crème	cream puff
shoo ah lah krem	
éclair *m* eh-klehr	long cake with a cream filling
mille-feuille *m* meel-fuh-yuh	Danish pastry with cream small cream puffs
profiteroles *f/pl*	cream puffs with chocolate or mocha cream
pro-fee-teh-rawl	
tarte *f* Tatin tahrt tahtaN	apple cake with caramel icing
tarte *f* aux fraises	strawberry tarts
tahrt oh frehz	
tuiles *f/pl* aux amandes	almond cookies
tweel o-zah-mahnd	

LISTE DES CONSOMMATIONS

Beverages

APÉRITIFS

Aperitifs

kir *m* keer	white wine with blackcurrant liqueur

kir *m* royal keer rwah-yahl	champagne with black-currant liqueur
pastis *m* pahs-teess	anisette-flavored liqueur

VINS

Wine

brut brew	dry (champagne)
champagne *m*	champagne
shaN-pahn-yuh	
cuvée *f* du patron	house wine
kew-veh dew pah-trohN	
(demi-)sec duh-mee sek	(medium) dry
doux doo	sweet
porto *m* paw-toh	port
vin *m* blanc vaN blahN	white wine
vin *m* de pays	locally-produced wine
vaN duh pay-ee	
vin *m* de table	table wine
vaN duh tah-bluh	
vin *m* d'appellation	high-quality wine
contrôlée vaN dah-pel-ah-	
see-ohN kohN-tro-lay	
vin *m* mousseux	sparkling wine
vaN moos-suh	
vin *m* rosé vaN ro-zeh	rosé wine
vin *m* rouge vaN roozh	red wine

AUTRES BOISSONS ALCOOLISÉES

Other Alcoholic Beverages

bière *f* bee-yehr	beer
bière *f* blonde	lager beer
bee-yehr blohNd	
bière *f* brune	dark beer
bee-yehr brewn	
bière *f* pression	draft beer
bee-yehr pres-see-ohN	
bière *f* sans alcool	non-alcoholic beer
bee-yehr sahN ahl-kawl	
calvados *m* kahl-vah-dawss	apple brandy
cassis *m* kah-seess	blackcurrant liqueur
cidre *m* see-druh	hard cider
digestif *m* dee-zhes-teef	digestive (brandy)
eau-de-vie *f* oh-duh-vee	spirits
marc *m* mahr	grappa, marc

BOISSONS NON ALCOOLISÉES

Non-alcoholic Beverages

citron *m* pressé	freshly squeezed lemon
see-trohN pres-say	juice
eau *f* minérale	mineral water
oh meen-eh-rahl	
eau *f* minérale gazeuse	carbonated mineral water
oh meen-eh-rahl gah-zuhz	
eau *f* minérale non gazeuse	non-carbonated
oh meen-eh-rahl nohN gah-zuhz	mineral water
grenadine *f* gruh-nah-deen	drink made from
	pomegranate syrup

jus *m* zhew	juice
jus *m* de pomme	apple juice
zhew duh pum	
jus *m* d'orange	orange juice
zhew daw-rahNzh	
limonade *f* lee-mo-nahd	lemonade
menthe *f* mahNt	peppermint syrup with water

BOISSONS CHAUDES

Hot Beverages.

café *m* kah-feh	coffee
café *m* au lait	coffee with milk
kah-feh oh leh	
café *m* crème kah-feh krem	coffee with foamed milk
café *m* express	espresso
kah-feh es-press	
chocolat *m* chaud	hot chocolate
sho-ko-lah sho	
infusion *f* aN-few-zee-ohN	herbal tea
infusion *f* de tilleul	linden blossom tea
aN-few-zee-ohN duh tee-uhl	
thé *m* teh	tea
thé *m* au citron	tea with lemon
teh oh see-trohN	
thé *m* au lait teh oh leh	tea with milk

Ordering

The menu, please.	La carte, s'il vous plaît.
	lah kahrt see voo play

 When asking for the waiter you say Monsieur! or, for the waitress, Mademoiselle!

I'd just like a snack.	Je voudrais seulement manger un petit quelque chose. zhuh voo-dray suhl-mahN mahN-zheh aN puh-tee kel-kuh shoze
Are you still serving hot meals?	Est-ce qu'on peut encore avoir quelque chose de chaud à manger? es kohN puh ahN-kaw ah-vwah kel-kuh shoze duh sho ah mahN-zheh
I'd just like something to drink.	Je voudrais seulement boire quelque chose. zhuh voo-dray suhl-mahN bwahr kel-kuh shoze
Are you still serving food?	Vous servez encore à manger ? voo sehr-veh ahN-kaw ah mahN-zheh
What do you recommend?	Que me recommandez-vous? kuh muh ruh-koh-mahN-day-voo
Que désirez-vous boire?	What would you like to drink?
Do you sell wine by the glass?	Avez-vous aussi du vin en carafe? ah-veh voo o-see dew vaN ahN kah-rahf

I'll have …

– a glass of red wine.

– a bottle of white wine.

– a carafe of house wine.

– a beer.

– a pitcher of water.

– some more bread.

– a *small* / *large* bottle of mineral water.

– a cup of coffee.

Je voudrais … zhuh voo-dray

– un verre de vin rouge.
aN vehr duh vaN roozh

– une bouteille de vin blanc.
ewn boo-teh-yuh duh vaN blahN

– une carafe de vin de la maison.
ewn kah-rahf duh vaN duh lah may-zohN

– une bière. ewn bee-yehr

– une carafe d'eau. ewn kah-rahf doh

– encore un peu de pain.
ahN-kaw aN puh duh paN

– une *petite* / *grande* bouteille d'eau minérale. ewn *puh-teet* / *grahNd* boo-teh-yuh doh meen-eh-rahl

– une tasse de café.
ewn tahss duh kah-feh

Que désirez-vous manger?

What would you like to eat?

I'll have …

– the … euro menu.

– a portion of …

– a piece of …

Je voudrais … zhuh voo-dray

– le menu à … euros.
luh muh-new ah … uh-roh

– une portion de …
ewn paw-see-ohN duh

– une part de … ewn pahr duh

What's today's special?

Quel est le plat du jour?
kel eh luh plah dew zhoor

What are the regional specialities here?

Quelles sont les spécialités de la région? kel sohN lay speh-see-ah-lee-teh duh lah ray-zhee-ohN

Eating and Drinking

Do you serve …	Avez-vous … ah-veh-voo
– diabetic meals?	– des plats pour diabétiques? day plah poor dee-ah-bay-teek
– dietary meals?	– des plats de régime? day plah duh ray-zheem
– vegetarian dishes?	– des plats végétariens? day plah veh-zheh-tah-ree-aN

Does it have … in it? I'm not allowed to eat any.	Est-ce qu'il y a … dans ce plat? Je n'ai pas le droit d'en manger. es keel ya … dahN suh plah zhuh nay pah luh drwah dahN mahN-zheh
Without … for me, please.	Pour moi sans …, s'il vous plaît. poor mwah sahN … see voo play
Comme *entrée* / *dessert*, qu'est-ce que vous prenez?	What would you like *as an appetizer* / *for dessert*?
I won't have *an appe-tizer* / *a dessert*, thank you.	Merci, je ne prends pas *d'entrée* / *de dessert*. mehr-see zhuh nuh prahN pah *dahN-treh* / *duh des-sehr*
Could I have … instead of …?	Est-ce que je pourrais avoir … au lieu de …? es kuh zhuh poor-eh ah-vwah … oh lyuh duh
Comment désirez-vous votre steak?	How would you like your steak?
Rare.	Saignant. sen-yahN
Medium.	A point. ah pwahN
Well done.	Bien cuit. bee-aN kwee

97

Complaints

That's not what I ordered. I wanted …	Ce n'est pas ce que j'ai commandé. Je voulais … suh neh pah suh kuh zheh kohN-mahN-day zhuh voo-lay
Have you forgotten my …?	Avez-vous oubliez ♂ mon / ♀ ma …? ah-veh-voo oo-blee-eh mohN / mah
There's / There are no …	Il n'y a pas de… eel nee ah pah duh
The food is *cold / too salty*.	Le repas est *froid / trop salé*. luh ruh-pah eh *frwah / tro sah-lay*
The meat isn't cooked through.	La viande n'est pas assez cuite. lah vee-ahNd neh pah-zah-say kweet
The meat's very tough.	La viande est dure. lah vee-ahNd eh dewr
Please take it back.	Remportez cela, s'il vous plaît. rahN-paw-teh suh-lah see voo play

► *Expressing Likes and Dislikes, page 19*

Paying

► *Numbers, see inside front cover*

The bill, please.	L'addition, s'il vous plaît. lah-dee-see-ohN see voo play
I'd like a receipt, please.	J'aimerais bien un reçu, s'il vous plaît. zhem-ehr-eh bee-aN aN ruh-sew see voo play

We'd like to pay separately.	Nous voudrions payer séparément. noo voo-dree-ohN pay-yeh say-pahr-eh-mahN
All together, please.	Une seule addition, s'il vous plaît. ewn suhl ah-dee-see-ohN see voo play
Vous êtes satisfait(s)?	Did you enjoy it?

Expressing Likes and Dislikes, page 19

Please give my compliments to the chef.	Mes compliments au chef de cuisine. may kohN-plee mahN oh shef duh kwee-zeen
I think there's been a mistake.	A mon avis, il y a une erreur. ah mohN ah-vee eel yah ewn eh-ruhr

info Service is generally included in the bill but if you are happy with the service a personal tip is appreciated—round the bill up 1-2 euros.

Having Lunch / Dinner Together

Enjoy your meal!	Bon appétit! bohN-nah-peh-tee
Cheers!	Santé! sahN-teh
Vous aimez ça?	Are you enjoying your meal?
It's very nice, thank you.	Merci, c'est très bon. mehr-see say treh bohN
Encore un peu de ...?	Would you like some more ...?
Yes, please.	Oui, volontiers. wee vol-ahN-tyeh

No thank you, I'm full.	Je n'ai plus faim, merci. zhuh nay plew faN mehr-see
What's that?	Qu'est-ce que c'est? kes kuh say
Could you pass me the …, please?	Vous pourriez me passer …, s'il vous plaît? voo poor-ee-eh muh pahs-say… see voo play
Do you mind if I smoke?	Ça vous dérange si je fume? sah voo day-rahNzh see zhuh fewm
Thank you very much for the invitation.	Merci pour l'invitation. mehr-see poor laN-vee-tah-see-ohN
It was excellent.	C'était excellent. say-teh ex-say-lahN

Eating and Drinking: Additional Words

appetizer	l'entrée *f* lahN-treh
ashtray	le cendrier luh sahN-dree-yeh
bar	le bistrot luh beess-tro
bottle	la bouteille lah boo-teh-yuh
bread	le pain luh paN
butter	le beurre luh buhr
chair	la chaise lah shez
cold	froid frwah
complete meal	le menu luh muh-new
course	le plat luh plah
cover charge	le couvert luh koo-vehr
cup	la tasse lah tahss
diet	le régime luh ray-zheem
dinner	le dîner luh dee-nay
dressing	la vinaigrette lah vee-neh-gret
drink	la boisson lah bwahs-sohN
fatty	gras *f*, grasse, *pl* grah grahss
fish bone	l'arête *f* lah-ret

food	le repas luh ruh-pah
fork	la fourchette lah foor-shet
fresh	frais *f*, fraîche, *pl* freh fresh
fruit	les fruits *m/pl* lay frwee
garlic	l'ail *m* lie
glass	le verre luh vehr
gravy	la sauce lah sohss
homemade	(fait) maison (feh) may-zohN
hot	chaud sho
hot (spicy)	épicé eh-pees-say
jam	la confiture lah koN-fee-tewr
ketchup	le ketchup luh ketch-up
knife	le couteau luh koo-toh
lean	maigre meh-gruh
light food	la cuisine diététique
	lah kwee-zeen dee-eh-teh-teek
lunch	le déjeuner luh day-zhuh-nay
main course	le plat de résistance
	luh plah duh ray-zees-tahNs
margarine	la margarine lah mahr-gahr-een
mayonnaise	la mayonnaise lah mah-yun-nez
meal	le plat *m* luh plah
mustard	la moutarde lah moo-tahrd
napkin	la serviette lah sehr-vyet
oil	l'huile *f* lweel
pasta	pâtes *f/pl* paht
(ground) pepper	le poivre luh pwahv-ruh
piece	le morceau luh maw-so
plate	l'assiette *f* lahs-syet
portion	la portion lah paw-see-ohN
potatoes	pommes *f/pl* de terre
	pum duh tehr
raw	cru crew
restaurant	le restaurant luh rest-o-rahN
rice	riz *m* ree

roll	le petit pain luh puh-tee paN
salad	salade *f* sah-lahd
salt	le sel luh sel
sandwich	le sandwich luh sahN-dweetch
sauce	la sauce lah sohss
seasoned	assaisonné ah-say-zohN-nay
service	le service luh sehr-veess
side dish	la garniture lah gahr-nee-tewr
silverware	les couverts *m/pl* lay koo-vehr
soup	le potage luh po-tahzh
sour	aigre eh-gruh
(sparkling / non-sparkling) mineral water	l'eau *f* minérale (gazeuse / non-gazeuse) lo mee-nay-rahl (gah-zuhz / nohN-gah-zuhz)
specialty	la spécialité lah speh-see-ah-lee-teh
spoon	la cuillère lah kwee-yehr
sugar	le sucre luh sew-kruh
sweet	sucré sew-cray
sweetener	la saccharine lah sahk-ah-reen
table	la table lah tah-bluh
tea	thé *m* teh
tip	le pourboire luh poor-bwahr
toothpick	le cure-dents luh kewr-dahN
vegetables (raw)	les crudités *f/pl* lay crew-dee-teh
vegetarian	végétarien veh-zheh-tah-ree-aN
vinegar	le vinaigre luh veen-eh-gruh
Waiter / Waitress	Monsieur / Mademoiselle moN-seeyew / mahd-mwah-sell
yogurt	le yaourt luh yah-oor

► *More Food Items, page 110*

Shopping

I'm just looking, thanks.
Merci, je regarde seulement.

How much is that?
Ça coûte combien?

Paying

How much is that?	Ça coûte combien? sah koot kohN-bee-aN
How much *is / are* …?	Combien *coûte / coûtent* …? kohN-bee-aN *koot / koot*
That's too expensive.	C'est trop cher pour moi. say tro shehr poor mwah
Can you come down a little?	Vous pouvez faire quelque chose pour le prix? voo poo-veh fehr kel-kuh shoze poor luh pree
Do I get a discount if I pay cash?	Vous me faites une réduction, si je paie en liquide? voo muh fet ewn ray-dewk-see-ohN see zhuh pay ahN lee-keed
Do you have anything on sale?	Vous avez des offres spéciales? voo-zah-veh day-zawf-fruh spay-see-ahl
Can I pay with this credit card?	Je peux payer avec (cette) carte de crédit? zhuh puh pay-yeh ah-vek (set) kahrt duh kray-dee
I'd like a receipt, please.	J'aimerais avoir une facture. zhem-eh-reh ah-vwahr ewn fahk-tewr

General Requests

Where can I get …?	Où est-ce que je peux acheter …? oo es kuh zhuh puh ahsh-teh
Vous désirez?	What would you like?
Je peux vous aider?	Can I help you?

104

I'm just looking, thanks.

Merci, je regarde seulement.
mehr-see zhuh ruh-gahrd suhl-mahN

I'm being helped, thanks.

Merci, on me sert.
mehr-see ohN me sehr

I'd like …

Je voudrais … zhuh voo-dreh

Je regrette, nous n'avons plus de …

I'm afraid we've run out of …

I don't like that so much.

Cela ne me plaît pas tellement.
suh-lah nuh muh play pah tel-mahN

Is there anything else you could show me?

Vous pourriez me montrer autre chose? voo poo-ree-eh muh mohN-tray o-truh shoze

I'll have to think about it.

Je dois encore réfléchir.
zhuh dwah ahN-kaw ray-fleh-sheer

I like that. I'll take it.

Cela me plaît. Je le prends.
suh-lah muh play zhuh luh prahN

Vous désirez encore quelque chose?

Anything else?

That's all, thanks.

Merci, ce sera tout.
mehr-see suh suh-rah too

Do you have a bag?

Vous auriez un sac?
voo-zo-ree-eh aN sahk

Could you wrap it up as a present, please?

Vous pourriez me faire un paquet cadeau? voo poo-ree-eh muh fehr aN pah-keh kah-doh

I'd like to *exchange* / *return* this.

Je voudrais *échanger* / *rendre* cela.
zhuh voo-dray *eh-shahN-zheh* / *rahN-druh* suh-lah

General Requests: Additional Words

(too) big	(trop) grand (tro) grahN
bigger	plus grand plew grahN
cheap(er)	(moins) cher (mwahN) shehr
check	le chèque luh shek
credit card	la carte de crédit
	lah kahrt duh kray-dee
end of season sales	les soldes *f/pl* lay sawld
(too) expensive	(trop) cher (tro) shehr
money	l'argent *m* lahr-zhahN
on sale	l'article *m* en promotion
	lahr-tee-kluh ahN pro-mo-see-ohN
receipt	le reçu luh ruh-sew
sale	les soldes *f/pl* lay sawld
self-service	le libre service
	luh lee-bruh sehr-veess
to buy	acheter ahsh-teh
to cost	coûter koo-teh
to return	rendre rahN-druh
to show	montrer mohN-tray
window display	la vitrine lah vee-treen

Shops and Stores

info Stores in France are generally open Monday through Saturday from 9 am to 7 pm. Some stores are closed during lunchtime, from 12-2 pm, except department stores or supermarkets. Most stores are closed on Sundays, some on Mondays as well.

antique shop	le magasin d'antiquités
	luh mah-gah-zaN dahN-tee-kee-teh
bakery	la boulangerie
	lah boo-lahN-zheh-ree
bookstore	la librairie lah lee-breh-ree
boutique	la boutique lah boo-teek
butcher's	la boucherie lah-boosh-uh-ree
candy store	la confiserie lah kohN-fee-suh-ree
chemist	la droguerie la drawg-uh-ree
delicatessen	l'épicerie *f* fine lay-pee-suh-ree feen
department store	le grand magasin
	luh grahN mah-gah-zaN
dry cleaner's	le pressing luh pres-sing
electronics store	le magasin d'électroménager
	luh mah-gah-zaN day-lek-tro-may-nah-zheh
fish store	la poissonnerie lay pwah-sun-uh-ree
florist	le fleuriste luh fluhr-eest
grocery store	l'épicerie *f* lay-pee-suh-ree
hairdresser	le coiffeur luh kwah-fur
hardware store	la quincaillerie lah kaN-kigh-uh-ree
jeweler's	le bijoutier luh bee-zhoo-tyeh
kiosk	le kiosque luh kee-awsk
laundromat	la laverie automatique
	lah lah-veh-ree o-toh-mah-teek

leather goods store	la maroquinerie
	lah mah-raw-keen-uh-ree
market	le marché luh mahr-sheh
music store	le magasin de musique
	luh mah-gah-zaN duh mew-zeek
newsstand	le marchand de journaux
	luh mahr-shahN duh zhoor-no
optician	l'opticien *m* lawp-tee-see-aN
pastry shop	la pâtisserie lah pah-tee-suh-ree
perfume shop	la parfumerie lah pah-few-muh-ree
pharmacy	la pharmacie lah fahr-mah-see
photo shop	le magasin d'articles
	photographiques luh mah-gah-
	zaN dahr-tee-kluh fo-toh-grah-feek
shoe repair shop	le cordonnier luh kaw-dohN-yeh
shoe store	le magasin de chaussures
	luh mah-gah-zaN duh sho-sewr
shopping center	le centre commercial
	luh sahN-truh kohN-mehr-see-ahl
souvenir shop	le magasin de souvenirs
	luh mah-gah-saN duh soo-ven-eer
sporting goods store	le magasin d'articles de sport luh
	mah-gah-zaN dahr-tee-kluh duh spawr
stationery store	la papeterie lah pahp-eh-tree
supermarket	le supermarché
	luh sew-pehr-mahr-sheh
tobacconist	le bureau de tabac
	luh bew-ro duh tah-bah
watch shop	l'horloger law-lo-zheh

Food

What's that?	Qu'est-ce que c'est? kes kuh say
Please give me …	Donnez-moi …, s'il vous plaît. dun-nay-mwah… see voo-play
– 100 grams (.022 lb) of …	– cent grammes de … sahN grahm duh
– a kilo (2.2 lbs) of …	– un kilo de … aN kee-lo duh
– a liter of …	– un litre de … aN lee-truh duh
– half a liter of …	– un demi-litre de … aN duh-mee lee-truh duh
– four slices of …	– quatre tranches de … kah-truh trahNsh duh
– a piece of …	– un morceau de … aN maw-so duh
A little *less* / *more*, please.	Un peu *moins* / *plus*, s'il vous plaît. aN puh *mwahN* / *plew* see voo play
Could I try some?	J'aimerais bien en essayer, s'il vous plaît? zhem-eh-reh bee-aN ahN es-eh-yeh see voo play

Food: Additional Words

alcohol-free beer	la bière sans alcool
	lah bee-yehr sahN-zahl-kawl
apple	la pomme lah pum
apple cider (alcoholic)	le cidre luh see-druh
apple juice	le jus de pomme luh zhew duh pum
apricot	l'abricot *m* lahb-ree-ko
artichoke	l'artichaut *m* lahr-tee-sho
asparagus	l'asperge *f* lah-spehrzh
avocado	l'avocat *m* lah-vo-kah
baby food	les aliments *m/pl* pour bébés
	lay-zah-lee-mahN poor bay-bay
balsamic vinegar	le vinaigre balsamique
	luh vee-nehg-ruh bahl-sah-meek
banana	la banane lah bah-nahn
basil	le basilic luh bah-see-leek
beans	les haricots *m/pl* lay ah-ree-ko
beef	le bœuf luh buhf
beer	la bière lah bee-yehr
bell pepper	le poivron luh pwah-vrohN
boiled ham	le jambon cuit luh zhahN-bohN kwee
bread	le pain luh paN
broccoli	le brocoli luh braw-kaw-lee
butter	le beurre luh buhr
cabbage	le chou luh shoo
cake	le gâteau luh gah-to
canned foods	les conserves *f/pl* lay kohN-sehrv
canned sardines	les sardines *f/pl* à l'huile
	lay sahr-deen ah lweel
carrots	les carottes *f/pl* lay kah-rawt
cereal	le muesli luh mews-lee
cheese	le fromage luh fro-mahzh
cherries	les cerises *f/pl* lay suh-reez
chicken	le poulet luh poo-lay

110

chicory	l'endive *f* lahN-deev
chili pepper	le piment luh pee-mahN
chives	les ciboulettes lay see-boo-let
chocolate	le chocolat luh sho-ko-lah
pork / lamb chop	la côtelette de porc / d'agneau
	lah kawt-uh-let duh pawr / dah-nyo
cocoa	le cacao luh kah-cow
coffee	le café luh kah-feh
cold cuts	la charcuterie lah shahr-kew-teh-ree
cookies	les biscuits *m/pl* lay beess-kwee
corn	le maïs luh mah-eess
cream	la crème lah krem
cucumber	le concombre luh kohN-kohN-bruh
(veal) cutlet	l'escalope *f* (de veau)
	less-kah-lawp (duh vo)
egg	l'œuf *m*, les œufs *pl* luhf, lay-zuh
eggplant	l'aubergine *f* lo-behr-zheen
fish	le poisson luh pwahs-sohN
fruit	les fruits *m/pl* lay frwee
garlic	l'ail *m* ligh
grapes	les raisins *m/pl* lay ray-saN
green beans	les haricots *m/pl* verts
	lay ah-ree-ko vehr
ground meat	la viande hachée lah
	vee-yahNd ash-eh
ham	le jambon luh zhahN-bohN
herbal tea	l'infusion *f* laN-few-zee-ohN
herbs	les fines herbes *f/pl* lay feen-zehrb
honey	le miel luh mee-yel
ice cream	la glace lah glahss
jam	la confiture lah kohN-fee-tewr
juice	le jus luh zhew
ketchup	le ketchup luh ketch-up
kiwi	le kiwi luh kee-vee
lamb	l'agneau *m* lahn-yo

leek	le poireau luh pwah-ro
lemon	le citron luh see-trohN
lettuce	la salade lah sah-lahd
liver pâté	le pâté de foie luh pah-teh duh fwah
lowfat milk	le lait demi-écrémé luh lay duh-mee eh-kray-may
margarine	la margarine lah mah-gah-reen
marmalade	la marmalade à l'orange la mahr-mah-lahd ah law-rahNzh
mayonnaise	la mayonnaise la mah-yuh-nez
meat	la viande lah vee-ahNd
melon	le melon luh muh-lohN
milk	le lait luh lay
mushrooms	les champignons *m/pl* lay shaN-peen-yohN
nectarine	la nectarine lah nek-tah-reen
nuts	les noix *f/pl* lay nwah
oil	l'huile *f* lweel
olive oil	l'huile d'olive lweel doh-leev
olives	les olives *f/pl* lay-zo-leev
onion	l'oignon *m* lohN-yohN
orange	l'orange *f* law-rahNzh
orange juice	le jus d'orange luh zhew daw-rahNzh
oregano	l'origan *m* law-ree-gahn
oysters	les huîtres *f/pl* lay weet-ruh
paprika	le piment luh pee-mahN
parsley	le persil luh pehr-see
pasta	les pâtes *f/pl* lay paht
peach	la pêche lah pehsh
peanuts	les cacahuètes *f/pl* lay kah-kah-wet
pear	la poire lah pwahr
peas	les petits pois *m/pl* lay puh-tee pwah
(ground) pepper	le poivre luh pwah-vruh

pepperoni	le salami luh sah-lah-mee
pickles	les cornichons *m/pl* lay kaw-nee-shohN
pineapple	l'ananas *m* lah-nah-nah
plums	les prunes *f/pl* lay prewn
pork	le porc luh pawr
potatoes	les pommes *f/pl* de terre lay pum duh tehr
poultry	la volaille lah vol-igh-yuh
raspberries	les framboises *f/pl* lay frahN-bwahz
red wine	le vin rouge luh vaN roozh
rice	le riz luh ree
roll	les petits pains *m/pl* lay puh-tee paN
rolled oats	les flocons *m/pl* d'avoine lay flaw-kohN dah-vwahn
rosemary	le romarin luh ro-mah-raN
rye bread	le pain noir luh paN nwahr
salt	le sel luh sel
sausages	la saucisse lah so-seess
semolina	la semoule lah suh-mool
smoked ham	le jambon cru luh zhahN-bohN krew
soda	la limonade lah lee-mo-nahd

sparkling / non-
  sparkling mineral
  water
	l'eau *f* minérale *gazeuse / non*
	  gazeuse lo meen-eh-rahl gah-zuhz /
	  nohN gah-zuhz

spices	les épices *f/pl* lay-zeh-peess
spinach	les épinards *m/pl* lay-zeh-pee-nahr
steak	le steak luh steak
strawberries	les fraises *f/pl* lay frez
sugar	le sucre luh sew-kruh
sweetener	la saccharine la sahk-ah-reen
tarragon	l'estragon *m* less-trah-gohN
tea	le thé luh teh
teabag	le sachet de thé luh sah-sheh duh teh

113

thyme	le thym luh taN
tomato	la tomate lah toh-maht
tuna	le thon luh tohN
veal	le veau luh vo
veal filet	l'escalope *f* less-kah-lawp
vegetables	les légumes *m/pl* lay lay-gewm
vinegar	le vinaigre luh vee-nehg-ruh
watermelon	la pastèque lah pahss-tek
white beans	les haricots *m/pl* blancs
	lay ah-ree-ko blahN
white bread	le pain blanc luh paN blahN
white wine	le vin blanc luh vaN blahN
whole grain bread	le pain complet luh paN kohN-pleh
wine	le vin luh vaN
without preservatives	sans agents *m/pl* de conservation
	sahN ah-zhahn duh kohN-sehr-vah-
	see-ohN
yogurt	le yaourt luh yah-oor
zucchini	la courgette lah koor-zhet

Souvenirs

I'd like …	Je voudrais … zhuh voo-dray
– a nice souvenir.	– un joli souvenir. aN zho-lee soo-ven-eer
– a present.	– un cadeau. aN kah-do
– something typical of the region.	– quelque chose de typique de la région. kel-kuh shoze duh tee-peek duh lah ray-zhee-ohN
Is this handmade?	Est-ce que c'est fait main? es-kuh say feh-maN
Is this *antique* / *genuine*?	Est-ce que c'est *ancien* / *du vrai*? es kuh say *ahN-see-aN* / *dew vreh*

Souvenirs: Additional Words

antique	l'antiquité *f* lahN-teek-kee-teh
arts and crafts	l'artisanat *m* lahr-tee-sahn-ah
belt	la ceinture lah saN-tewr
beret	le béret (basque) luh bay-ray (bahsk)
blanket	la couverture lah koo-vehr-tewr
bowl (salad)	le saladier luh sah-lahd-yeh
bowl	le bol luh bawl
certificate	le certificat luh sehr tee-fee-kah
crockery, tableware	la vaisselle lah veh-sel
cup, goblet	le gobelet luh gawb-lay
cup, mug	la tasse la tahss
hand-carved	sculpté à la main scewlp-teh ah lah maN
handmade	fait à la main feh ah maN
handpainted	peint à la main paN ah lah maN
jewelry	les bijoux *m/pl* lay bee-zhoo
jug	le broc luh brawk

lace	la dentelle lah dahN-tel
lavender	la lavande la lah-vahNd
leather	le cuir luh kweer
pottery	la poterie lah paw-tuh-ree
pottery, ceramics	la céramique la seh-rah-meek
purse, handbag	le sac à main luh sahk ah maN
silk scarf	le foulard en soie
	luh foo-lahr ahN swah
souvenir	le souvenir luh soo-ven-eer
special blend of herbs from the Provence region	les herbes *f/pl* de Provence lay-zehrb duh pro-vahNs
stoneware	la faïence lah figh-yahNs
tablecloth	la nappe la nahp
terracotta	la terre cuite la tehr kweet
vase	le vase luh vahz

Clothing

Buying Clothes

I'm looking for …   Je cherche … zhuh shehrsh

Quelle est votre   What size are you?
taille?

I'm (US) size …   Ma taille (américaine) est …
                             mah tigh-yuh (ah-meh-ree-ken) eh

info

	Dresses/Suits						Shirts			
American	8	10	12	14	16	18	15	16	17	18
British	10	12	14	16	18	20				
Continental	38	40	42	44	46	48	38	41	43	45

Do you have it in   Est-ce que vous l'avez aussi dans la
a size …?   taille…? es kuh voo lah-veh o-see
                             dahN lah tigh-yuh…

Do you have it in a   Est-ce que vous l'avez aussi dans
different color?   une autre couleur? es kuh voo lah-
                             veh o-see dahN-zewn o-truh koo-luhr

▶ Colors, page 119

Could I try this on?   Je peux l'essayer?
                             zhuh puh less-eh-yeh

Where is there a   Où est le miroir? oo eh luh meer-wahr
mirror?

Where are the fitting   Où sont les cabines d'essayage?
rooms?   oo sohN lay kah-been dess-eh-yahzh

What fabric is this?	C'est quoi comme tissu?
	say kwah kom tees-sew
It doesn't fit me.	Cela ne me va pas.
	suh-lah nuh muh vah pah
It's too *big / small*.	C'est trop *grand / petit*.
	say tro *grahN / puh-tee*
It fits nicely.	Cela va parfaitement.
	suh-lah vah pahr-fet-mahN

Laundry and Dry Cleaning

I'd like this dry-cleaned.	Je voudrais faire nettoyer cela. zhuh voo-dreh fehr net-twah-yeh suh-lah
Could you remove this stain?	Vous pouvez enlever cette tache? voo poo-veh ahN-luh-vay set tahsh
When can I pick it up?	Quand est-ce que je peux venir le reprendre? kahN-tes kuh zhuh puh ven-eer luh ruh-pahN-druh

Fabrics and Materials

camel hair	le poil de chameau
	luh pwahl duh shah-mo
cashmere	le cachemire luh kahsh-meer
cotton	le coton luh koh-tohN
fleece	la fibre polaire la fee-bruh po-lehr
lambswool	le mohair luh mo-hehr
leather	le cuir luh kweer
linen	le lin luh laN
man-made fiber	le synthétique luh saN-teh-teek
microfiber	la microfibre lah mee-kro-fee-bruh

118

natural fiber   les fibres *f/pl* naturelles
                       lay fee-bruh nah-tewr-el
pure new wool   la pure laine vierge
                       lah pewr len vee-yerzh
silk   la soie   la swah
suede   le chamois   luh shah-mwah
wool   la laine   lah len

Colors

beige   beige   behzh
black   noir   nwahr
blue   bleu   bluh
brown   marron   mah-rohN
burgundy   rouge foncé   roozh fohN-say
colorful   multicolore   mewl-tee-ko-lawr
golden   doré   daw-ray
gray   gris   gree
green   vert   vehr
light blue   bleu ciel   bluh see-yel
navy blue   bleu marine   bluh mah-reen
pink   rose   rohz
purple   violet   vee-o-lay
red   rouge   roozh
silver   argent   ahr-zhahN
solid-color   uni   ew-nee
turquoise   turquoise   tewr-kwahz
white   blanc *m*, blanche *f*   blahN blahnsh
yellow   jaune   zhone

Clothing: Additional Words

anorak	l'anorak *m* lah-naw-rahk
bathing suit	le maillot de bain
	luh ma-yoh duh baN
bathrobe	le peignoir (de bain)
	luh pen-ywahr (duh baN)
beach hat	le chapeau de soleil
	luh shah-po-duh so-lay
belt	la ceinture lah san-tewr
bikini	le bikini luh bee-kee-nee
blazer	le blazer luh blah-zehr
blouse	le chemisier luh shuh-mee-zee-yeh
bra	le soutien-gorge
	luh soo-tee-aN gawrzh
briefs	le slip luh sleep
cap	le bonnet luh bun-eh
coat	le manteau luh mahN-toh

dress	la robe lah rawb
gloves	les gants *m/pl* lay gahN
hat	le chapeau luh shah-po
jacket	la veste lah vest
jeans	le jean luh jean
long	long lohN
long sleeves	les manches *f/pl* longues lay mahNsh lohNg
pajamas	le pyjama luh pee-dzhah-mah
panties	la culotte lah kew-lawt
pants	le pantalon luh pahN-tah-lohN
pantyhose	le collant luh ko-lahN
raincoat	l'imperméable *m* laN-pehr-may-ah-bluh
scarf	l'écharpe *f* lay-shahrp
shirt	la chemise lah shmeez
short	court koor
short sleeves	les manches courtes *f/pl* lay mahNsh koort
shorts	le short luh shawr
skirt	la jupe lah jewp
socks	les chaussettes *f/pl* lay sho-set
sports jacket	le veston luh ves-tohN
stockings	les mi-bas *m/pl* lay mee-bah
suit	le costume luh kaw-stewm
suit	le tailleur luh ta-yuhr
sweater	le pullover luh pewl-oh-vehr
swimming trunks	le caleçon de bain luh kahl-sohN duh baN
T-shirt	le T-shirt luh tee shert
tie	la cravate lah krah-vaht
track pants	le pantalon de jogging luh pahN-tah-lohN duh zhawg-ing
tracksuit	la tenue de jogging lah tuh-new duh zhawg-ing

undershirt	le maillot de corps
	luh mah-yot duh kawr
underwear	les dessous *m/pl* lay des-soo
vest	le gilet luh zhee-lay
wrinkle-free	infroissable aN-frwah-sah-bluh
zipper	la fermeture éclaire
	lah fehr-meh-tewr eh-klehr

In the Shoe Store

I'd like a pair of …	Je voudrais une paire de …
	zhuh voo-dreh ewn pehr duh
Quelle est votre pointure?	What's your shoe size?
I wear size …	Je porte du … zhuh pawrt dew
The heels are too *high / low*.	Le talon est trop *haut / plat*.
	luh tah-lohN eh tro *oh / plah*
They're too *big / small*.	Elles sont trop *grandes / petites*.
	el sohN tro *grahNd / puh-teet*
They're tight around here.	Elles me serrent ici.
	el muh sehr ee-see

info

	Women's Shoes	Men's Shoes
American	6 7 8 9	6 7 8 8½ 9 9½ 10 11
British	4½ 5½ 6½ 7½	
Continental	37 38 39 40	38 39 40 41 42 43 44 44

Shoe Store: Additional Words

boots	les bottes *f/pl* lay bawt
flip-flops	les sandales *f/pl* de bain
	lay sahN-dahl duh baN
high heels	les escarpins *m/pl*
	lay-zess-kahr-paN
hiking boots	les chaussures *f/pl* de montagne
	lay sho-sewr duh mohN-tahn-yuh
insoles	les semelles *f/pl* lay suh-mel
leather	le cuir luh kweer
leather sole	la semelle en cuir
	la suh-mel ahN kweer
rubber boots	les bottes *f/pl* en caoutchouc
	lay bawt ahN kah-oo-kshoo
sandals	les sandales *f/pl* lay sahN-dahl
shoe polish	le cirage luh see-rahzh
shoelaces	les lacets *m/pl* lay lah-say
shoes	les chaussures *f/pl* lay sho-sewr
size	la pointure lah pwaN-tewr
sneakers	les baskets *m/pl* lay bahs-keh
suede	le chamois luh shah-mwah
tight	serré sehr-ray
walking shoes	les chaussures *f/pl* de randonnée
	lay sho-sewr duh rahN-dun-eh

Jewelry and Watches

I need a new battery for my watch.	J'ai besoin d'une pile neuve pour cette montre. zhay buh-swaN dewn peel nuhv poor set mohN-truh

I'm looking for a nice souvenir / present.	Je cherche un joli *souvenir / cadeau.* zhuh shehrsh aN zho-lee *soo-ven-eer / kah-doh*
Dans quel prix?	How much do you want to spend?
What's this made of?	C'est en quoi? say ahN kwah

Jewelry and Watches: Additional Words

alarm clock	le réveil luh ray-veh
bracelet	le bracelet luh brahss-lay
brooch	la broche lah brawsh
carat	le carat luh kah-rah
clip-on earrings	les boucles *f/pl* d'oreille à clips lay boo-kluh daw-ray ah kleep
costume jewelry	le bijou fantaisie luh bee-zhoo fahN-teh-zee
diamond	le diamant luh dee-ah-mahN
earrings	les boucles *f/pl* d'oreille lay boo-kluh daw-ray
gold	l'or *m* lawr
gold-plated	doré daw-ray
jewelry	les bijoux *m/pl* lay bee-zhoo
necklace	la chaîne lah shen
pearl	la perle lah pehrl
pendant	le pendentif luh pahN-dahN-teef
platinum	le platine luh plah-teen
ring	la bague lah bahg
silver	l'argent *m* lah-zhahN
watch	la montre lah mohN-truh
watchband	le bracelet de montre luh brahss-lay duh mohN-truh

Health and Beauty

adhesive bandage	le pansement adhésif
	luh pahNs-mahN ah-day-seef
baby powder	la poudre pour bébés
	lah poo-druh poor bay-bay
barrette	la barrette lah bah-ret
blush	le blush luh blush
body lotion	la lotion corporelle
	lah lo-see-ohN kor-por-el
brush	la brosse lah brawss
comb	le peigne luh pen-yuh
condoms	les préservatifs *m/pl*
	lay pray-sehr-vah-teef
cotton balls	le coton luh co-tohN
cotton swabs	les Cotons-Tiges® *m/pl*
	lay co-tohN-teeg
dental floss	le fil dentaire luh feel dahN-tehr
deodorant	le déodorant luh day oh-daw-rahN
detergent	le détergent luh day-tehr-zhahN
(elastic) hairband	l'élastique *m* à cheveux
	lay-lahs-teek ah shuh-vuh
eye shadow	l'ombre *f* à paupières
	lohN-bruh ah po-pyehr
eyeliner	le crayon khôl luh cray-ohN kohl
face wash	le lait démaquillant
	luh lay day-mah-kee-yahN
fragrance-free	non parfumé nohN pahr-few-may
hairclips	les pinces *f/pl* à cheveux
	lay paNs ah shuh-vuh
hairspray	la laque à cheveux
	lah lahk ah shuh-vuh
hand cream	la crème de soins pour mains
	lah krem duh swan poor maN

hypoallergenic	hypoallergènique ee-poh-ahl-ehr-zheh-neek
lip balm	le stick à lèvres luh steek ah leh-vruh
lipstick	le rouge à lèvres luh roozh ah leh-vruh
mascara	le rimmel luh ree-mel
mirror	le miroir luh meer-wahr
moisturizer	la crème de jour lah krem duh zhoor
mosquito repellent	la protection anti-moustiques lah pro-tek-see-ohN ahN-tee-moo-steek
mousse	la mousse renforçatrice lah mooss rahN-faw-sah-treess
nail file	la lime à ongles lah leem ah ohN-gluh
nail polish	le vernis à ongles luh vehr-nee ah ohN-gluh
nail polish remover	le dissolvant luh dee-sawl-vahN
nail scissors	les ciseaux *m/pl* à ongles lay see-zo ah ohN-gluh
nailbrush	la brosse à ongles lah brawss ah ohN-gluh
night cream	la crème de nuit lah krem duh nwee
perfume	le parfum luh pahr-faN
razor blade	la lame de rasoir lah lahm duh rah-swah
sanitary napkins	les serviettes *f/pl* hygiéniques lay sehrv-yet hee-zhen-eek
shampoo	le shampooing luh shahN-pwaN
shaving cream	la mousse à raser lah mooss ah rah-zeh
shower gel	le gel douche luh zhel doosh
soap	le savon luh sah-vohN
styling gel	le gel coiffant luh zhel kwah-fahN
sun protection factor (SPF)	le facteur de protection solaire luh fahk-tuhr duh pro-tek-see-ohN so-lehr
sunscreen	la crème solaire lah krem so-lehr

suntan lotion	le lait solaire luh lay so-lehr
tampons	les tampons *m/pl* lay tahN-pohN
tissues	les mouchoirs *m/pl* en papier
	lay moosh-wahr ahN pah-pyeh
toilet paper	le papier hygiénique
	luh pah-pyeh hee-zhen-eek
toothbrush	la brosse à dents lah brawss ah dahN
toothpaste	le dentifrice luh dahN-tee-freess
toothpicks	le cure-dents luh kewr-dahN
tweezers	la pince à épiler
	lah paNs ah eh-pee-lay
washcloth	le gant de toilette
	luh gahN duh twah-let
wipes	les lingettes *f/pl* lay laN-zhet

Household Articles

aluminum foil	l'aluminium *m* ménager
	lahl-meen-yum may-nah-zheh
bottle opener	le décapsuleur luh day kahp-sewl-uhr
broom	le balai luh bah-lay
bucket	le seau luh soh
can opener	l'ouvre-boîte *m* loo-vruh bwaht
candles	les bougies *f* lay boo-zhee
charcoal	le charbon de bois
	luh shahr-bohN duh bwah
cleaning products	les produits *m/pl* de nettoyage
	lay pro-dwee duh net-wah-yazh
cloth	le chiffon luh shee-fohN
clothes pins	les pinces *f/pl* à linge
	lay paNs ah laNzh
cooler	la glacière la glah-syehr
corkscrew	le tire-bouchon luh teer-boo-shohN
cup	la tasse lah tahss

detergent	la lessive lah les-seev
dishtowel	la lavette lah lah-vet
dishwashing detergent	le liquide vaisselle
	luh lee-keed veh-sel
fork	la fourchette lah foor-shet
frying pan	la poêle lah pwahl
glass	le verre luh vehr
grill lighter	l'allume-feu *m* lahl-ewm-fuh
insect spray	le spray anti-insectes
	luh spreh ahN-tee aN-sekt
knife	le couteau luh koo-to
laundry line	la corde à linge lah kord ah laNzh
light bulb	l'ampoule *f* lahN-pool
lighter	le briquet luh bree-keh
matches	les allumettes *f/pl* lay-zahl-ew-met
methylated spirits	l'alcool *m* à brûler
	lahl-kawl ah brew-lay
mosquito coil	la spirale anti-moustiques
	lah spee-rahl ahN-tee-moo-steek
napkins	les serviettes *f/pl* lay sehr-vyet
paper towels	le rouleau de papier (absorbant)
	luh roo-lo duh pah-pyeh (ahb-sawr-bahN)
plastic cup	le gobelet en plastique
	luh gawb-lay ahN plah-steek
plastic plate	l'assiette *f* en plastique
	lahs-syet ahN plah-steek
plastic utensils	les couverts *m/pl* en plastique
	lay koo-vehr ahN plah-steek
plastic wrap	le film fraîcheur luh feelm freh-shuhr
plate	l'assiette *f* lah-syet
pocket knife	le couteau de poche
	luh koo-toh duh pawsh
safety pin	l'épingle *f* de sûreté
	lay-paN-gluh duh sewr-teh

saucepan	la casserole lah kahss-rawl
scissors	les ciseaux *m/pl* lay see-zo
sewing needle	l'aiguille *f* à coudre
	lay-gwee ah koo-druh
sewing thread	le fil à coudre luh feel ah koo-druh
spoon	la cuillère lah kwee-yehr
stain remover	le détachant luh day-tahsh-mahN

Electrical Articles

adapter	l'adaptateur *m* lah-dahp-tah-tuhr
alarm clock	le réveil luh ray-veh
battery	la pile lah peel
extension cord	la rallonge lah rah-lohNzh
flashlight	la lampe de poche
	lah lahNp duh pawsh
immersion heater	le thermoplongeur
	luh tehr-mo-plohN-zhuhr
pocket calculator	la calculette lah kahl-kew-let
razor	le rasoir luh rah-swah

At the Optician

My glasses are broken.	Mes lunettes sont cassées. may lew-net sohN kah-say
Can you repair this?	Pouvez-vous réparer cela? poo-veh voo ray-pah-ray suh-lah
I'd like some disposable lenses.	J'aimerais avoir des lentilles journalières jetables. zhem-eh-reh ah-vwahr day lahN-tee-yuh zhoor-nahl-yehr zhuh-tah-bluh

Avez-vous un carnet pour *les lunettes* / *lentilles*?	Do you have a *glasses* / *contact lens* prescription card?
Combien de dioptries avez-vous?	What's your prescription?
I've got … dioptres in the left eye and … dioptres in the right.	J'ai … dioptries à gauche et … dioptries à droite. zheh … dee-awp-tree ah gosh eh … dee-awp-tree ah drwaht
I've *lost* / *broken* a contact lens.	J'ai *perdu* / *cassé* une lentille (de contact). zheh *pehr-dew* / *kah-say* ewn lahN-tee-yuh (duh kohN-tahkt)
I need some saline solution for *hard* / *soft* contact lenses.	Il me faudrait une solution de conservation pour lentilles *dures* / *souples*. eel muh fo-dreh ewn so-lew-see-ohN duh kohN-sehr-vah-see-ohN poor lahN-tee-yuh *dewr* / *soo-pluh*
I need some cleaning solution for *hard* / *soft* contact lenses.	Il me faudrait une solution de nettoyage pour lentilles *dures* / *souples*. eel muh fo-dreh ewn so-lew-see-ohN duh net-twah-yahzh poor lahN-tee-yuh *dewr* / *soo-pluh*
I'd like a pair of sunglasses.	Je voudrais des lunettes de soleil. zhuh voo-dreh day lew-net duh so-lay

At the Photo Store

I'd like …	Je voudrais … zhuh-voo-dreh
– a memory card for this camera.	– une carte mémoire pour cet appareil. ewn kahrt mehm-wahr poor set ahp-pah-ray
– film for this camera.	– une pellicule pour cet appareil. ewn pel-ee-cewl poor set ahp-pah-ray
– color film.	– un film (négatif en couleurs). aN feelm (nay-gah-teef ahN koo-luhr)
– slide film.	– une pellicule pour diapositives. ewn pel-ee-kewl poor dee-ah-pos-ee-teev
– 24 / 36-exposure film.	– une pellicule de vingt-quatre / trente-six expositions. ewn pel- lee-kewl duh vaNt-kah-truh / trahNt- seess ex-po-zee-see-ohN
I'd like some batteries for this camera.	Je voudrais des piles pour cet appareil. zhuh voo-dreh day peel poor set ahp-pah-ray
Could you put the film in for me, please?	Vous pouvez me placer la pellicule dans l'appareil, s'il vous plaît? voo-poo-veh muh plah-say lah pel-ee-kewl dahN lah-pah-ray see voo play
When will the prints be ready?	Les photos seront prêtes quand? lay fo-toh suh-rohN pret kahN
Can you repair my camera?	Vous pouvez réparer mon appareil photo? voo poo-veh ray-pah-ray mohN ahp-pah-ray fo-toh
It won't advance.	Il bloque. eel blawk

The shutter release / The flash doesn't work.	*Le déclencheur / Le flash* ne fonctionne pas. *luh day-clahN-shuhr / luh flahsh nuh fohNk-see-on pah*
I'd like to have some passport photos taken.	Je voudrais faire faire des photos d'identité. *zhuh voo-dreh fehr fehr day fo-toh dee-dahN-tee-teh*

Photo Store: Additional Words

camcorder	le caméscope *luh kahm-eh-skawkp*
CD / DVD	le *CD / DVD* *luh say-day / day-veh-day*
digital camera	l'appareil *m* photo numérique *lah-pah-ray fo-toh new-mehr-eek*
exposure meter	le posemètre *luh pohs-meh-truh*
(film) speed	la sensibilité *lah saN-see-bee-lee-teh*
film camera	la caméra *lah kah-meh-rah*
filter	le filtre *luh feel-truh*
flash	le flash *luh flahsh*
lens	l'objectif *m* *lawb-zhek-teef*
negative	le négatif *luh nay-gah-teef*
photo	la photo *la fo-toh*
self-timer	le déclencheur automatique *luh day-klahN-shuhr o-toh-mah-teek*
SLR camera	le réflex *luh ray-flex*
telephoto lens	le téléobjectif *luh teh-lay-awb-zhek-teef*
UV filter	le filtre UV *luh feel-truh ew-veh*
video camera	la caméra vidéo *lah kahm-eh-rah vee-day-o*
video cassette	la vidéocassette *lah vee-day-o-kahs-set*
wide-angle lens	l'objectif *m* grand angle *lawb-zhek-teef grahn-than-gluh*
zoom lens	le zoom *luh zoom*

At the Music Store

Do you have any CDs by …?
Vous avez des CDs de …?
voo-zah-veh day say-day duh

I'd like a CD of traditional French music.
J'aimerais bien un CD de musique française *traditionelle / folklorique*.
zhem-eh-reh bee-aN aN say-day duh mew-zeek frahN-seh-zhuh *trah-dee-see-ohN-el / fawlk-law-reek*

Music: Additional Words

cassette	la cassette	lah kah-set
headphones	les écouteurs	lay-zeh-koo-tuhr
music	la musique	lah mew-zeek
radio	la radio	lah rah-dee-oh
Walkman®	le baladeur	luh bah-lah-duhr

Books and Stationery

I'd like …
Je voudrais … zhuh voo-dreh

– an American newspaper.
– un journal américain.
aN zhoor-nahl ah-may-ree-kaN

– an American magazine.
– un magazine américain.
aN mah-gah-zeen ah-may-ree-kaN

– a map of the area.
– une carte de la région.
ewn kahrt duh lah ray-zhee-ohN

– a map of the town.
– un plan de la ville.
aN plahN duh lah veel

Do you have a more recent paper?
Vous auriez aussi un journal plus récent? voo-zo-ree-eh oh-see aN zhoor-nahl plew ray-sahN

133

Do you have any English books?	Est-ce que vous avez des livres anglais? es-kuh voo-zah-veh day lee-vruh ahN-gleh

Books and Stationery: Additional Words

ballpoint pen	le stylo bille luh stee-lo beel
cookbook	le livre de cuisine luh lee-vruh duh kwee-zeen
detective novel	le policier luh paw-lee-see-eh
dictionary	le dictionnaire luh deek-see-ohN-nehr
envelope	l'enveloppe *f* lahN-vel-awp
eraser	la gomme lah gawm
felt tip	le feutre luh fuh-truh
glue	la colle lah cawl

hiking map	la carte de randonnées pédestres
	  lah kahrt duh rahN-dun-eh pay-des-
	  truh

magazine	le magazine illustré *m* luh mah-gah-zeen ee-lew-stray
map of cycling routes	la carte de randonnées cyclistes lah kahrt duh rahN-dun-eh see-kleest
novel	le roman luh ro-mahN
paper	le papier luh pahp-yeh
pencil	le crayon luh cray-ohN
pencil sharpener	le taille-crayon luh tigh-cray-ohN
playing cards	les cartes *f/pl* à jouer lay kahrt ah zhoo-eh
postcard	la carte postale lah kahrt pos-tahl
printer cartridge	la cartouche d'imprimante lah kahr-toosh daN-pree-mahNt
road map	la carte routière lah kahrt roo-tyehr

travel guide	le guide de voyage
	luh geed duh vwah-ahzh
tape	le ruban adhésif
	luh rew-bahN ahd-eh-seef
writing pad	le bloc-notes luh blawk-noht
writing paper	le papier à lettres
	luh pahp-yeh ah leh-truh

At the Tobacco Shop

A pack of cigarettes *with* / *without* filters, please.

Un paquet de cigarettes *avec* / *sans* filtres, s'il vous plaît. aN pah-keh duh see-gah-ret *ah-vek* / *sahN* feel-truh see voo play

A *pack* / *carton* of …, please.

Un paquet / *Une cartouche* de …, s'il vous plaît. *aN pah-keh* / *ewn kahr-toosh* duh… see voo play

Are these cigarettes *strong* / *mild*?

Ces cigarettes sont *fortes* / *légères*? say see-gah-ret sohN *fawrt* / *lay-zhehr*

A pouch of *pipe* / *cigarette* tobacco, please.

Un paquet de tabac *pour pipe* / *à cigarettes*, s'il vous plaît. aN pah-keh duh tah-bah *poor peep* / *ah see-gah-ret* see voo play

Could I have a *lighter* / *book of matches*, please?

Un briquet / *Une boîte d'allumettes*, s'il vous plaît. *aN bree-keh* / *ewn bwaht dahl-ewm-et* see voo play

Tobacco: Additional Words

cigarillos	les cigarillos *m/pl*
	lay see-gah-ree-yo
cigars	les cigares *m/pl* llay see-gahr
pipe	la pipe lah peep
pipe cleaner	le cure-pipe luh kewr-peep

Sports and Leisure

How do we get to the beach?
Comment va-t-on à la plage?

I'd like to rent a bicycle.
Je voudrais louer un vélo.

Activities

Beach and Pool

How do we get to the beach?	Comment va-t-on à la plage? kohN-mahN vah-tohN ah lah plahzh
Is swimming permitted here?	On peut se baigner ici? ohN puh suh ben-yeh ee-see
Are there (strong) currents around here?	Y a-t'il des courants (forts) ici? ee-ah-teel day- koo-rahN (fawr) ee-see
When is *low / high* tide?	Quelle est l'heure de la marée *basse / haute*? kel eh luhr duh lah mah-ray *bahss / oht*
Are there jellyfish around here?	Est-ce qu'il y a des méduses ici? es keel ya day may-dews ee-see
I'd like to rent …	Je voudrais louer … zhuh voo-dreh loo-eh
– a deckchair.	– une chaise longue. ewn shehz lohNg
– an umbrella.	– un parasol. aN pah-rah-sawl
– a boat.	– un bateau. aN bah-to
I'd like to take a *diving / windsurfing* course.	Je veux bien reçevoir des instructions *de plongée / de windsurf*. zhuh vuh bee-aN ruh-suh-vvahr day-zaN-strewk-see-ohn *duh plohN-zheh / duh wind-surf*
How much is it per *hour / day*?	Quel est le tarif pour *une heure / une journée*? kel eh luh tah-reef poor *ewn uhr / ewn zhoor-nay*

Would you mind watching my things for a moment, please?	Vous pourriez surveiller mes affaires un instant, s'il vous plaît? voo poor-ee-eh sewr-veh-yeh may-zah-fehr aN-naN-stahN see voo play
Is there an indoor / outdoor pool here?	Est-ce qu'il y a une piscine couverte / découverte ici? es keel yah ewn pee-seen koo-vehrt / day-koo-vehrt ee-see
What change do I need for the lockers / hair dryers?	Pour le vestiaire / sèche-cheveux, qu'est-ce qu'il me faut comme pièces? poor luh ves-tyehr / sehsh-shuh-vuh kes-keel muh fo kum pee-yes
I'd like to rent / buy ...	Je voudrais louer / acheter ... zhuh voo-dreh loo-eh / ahsh-teh
– a swimming cap.	– un bonnet de bain. aN bun-eh duh baN
– swimming goggles.	– des lunettes de piscine. day lewn-et duh pee-seen
– towel.	– une serviette de bain. ewn sehr-vyet duh baN
Where's the pool attendant / first-aid station?	Où est le maître-nageur / poste de secours? oo eh luh meh-truh-nah-zhuhr / pawst duh suh-koor

Beach and Pool: Additional Words

arm floats	les brassards m/pl de natation lay brah-sahr duh nah-tah-see-ohN
beach	la plage lah plahzh
beach ball	le ballon de plage luh bah-lohN duh plahzh

boat rentals	la location de bateaux
	lah lo-kah-see-ohN duh bah-to
changing room	la cabine lah kah-been
to dive	plonger plohN-zheh
diving equipment	l'équipement *m* de plongée
	lay-keep-mahN duh plohN-zheh
diving mask	les lunettes *f/pl* de plongée
	lay lewn-et duh plohN-zheh
to fish	pêcher peh-sheh
flippers	les palmes *f/pl* lay pahlm
high tide	la marée haute lah mah-ray oht
jet ski	le scooter des mers
	luh skoo-tuhr day mehr
lake	le lac luh lahk
life preserver	la bouée de sauvetage
	lah boo-eh duh sohv-tahzh
low tide	la marée basse lah mah-ray bahss
motorboat	le bateau à moteur
	luh bah-to ah mo-tuhr
non-swimmers	le non-nageur luh nohN-nah-zhuhr
nude beach	la plage naturiste
	lah plahzh nah-tew-reest
ocean	la mer lah mehr
pedal boat	le pédalo luh pay-dah-lo
row boat	le bateau à rames
	luh bah-to ah rahm
(rubber) raft	le bateau pneumatique
	luh bah-to pnuh-mah-teek
to sail	faire de la voile fehr duh lah vwahl
sail boat	le voilier luh vwahl-yeh
sand	le sable luh sah-bluh
sea urchin	l'oursin *m* loor-saN
shade	l'ombre *f* lohN-bruh
shells	les coquillages *m/pl*
	lay co-kee-yahzh

shower	la douche lah doosh
snorkel	le tube de plongée
	luh tewb duh plohN-zheh
storm warning	l'avis *m* de tempête
	lah-vee duh tahN-pet
sun	le soleil luh so-lay
sunglasses	les lunettes *f/pl* de soleil
	lay lewn-et duh so-lay
sunscreen	la crème solaire lah krem so-lehr
surfboard	la planche à voile
	lah plahNsh ah vwahl
to swim, bathe	se baigner suh ben-yeh
to swim	nager nah-zheh
swimming area	la plage gardée lah plahzh gahr-day
swimming pool	la piscine lah pee-seen
water	l'eau *f* lo
water ski	le ski nautique luh ski no-teek
wave	la vague lah vahg
wave pool	la piscine à vagues
	lah pee-seen ah vahg

Games

Do you mind if I join in?	Je peux jouer avec vous? zhuh puh zhoo-eh ah-vek voo
We'd like to rent a squash court for (half) an hour.	Nous voudrions retenir un court de squash pour une (demi-)heure. noo voo-dree-ohN ruh-ten-eer aN koor duh squash poor ewn (duh-mee) uhr
We'd like to rent a tennis court for an hour.	Nous voudrions retenir un court de tennis pour une heure. noo voo-dree-ohN ruh-ten-eer aN koor duh ten-neess poor ewn uhr
Where can you *go bowling / play pool* here?	Oú es-ce qu'on peut jouer au *bowling / billard*? oo es kohN puh zhoo-eh o *bowling / bee-yahr*
I'd like to rent …	Je voudrais louer … zhuh voo-dreh loo-eh

Games: Additional Words

badminton	le badminton luh bahd-mee-tohN
badminton racket	la raquette de badminton lah rah-ket duh bahd-meen-tohN
ball	un ballon aN bah-lohN
basketball	le basket luh bahs-ket
beach volleyball	le beach-volley luh beach-vawl-eh
bowling alley	le bowling luh bow-ling
double	le double luh doo-bluh
game	le jeu luh zhuh
goal	les buts *m/pl* lay bew
goalkeeper	le gardien de but luh gahr-dee-aN duh bew
golf	le golf luh gawlf

golf ball	la balle de golf	lah bahl duh gawlf
golf club	le club de golf	luh cluhb duh gawlf
golf course	le terrain de golf	
		luh tehr-raN duh gawlf
handball	le handball	luh ahNd-bahl
to lose	perdre	pehr-druh
miniature golf course	le mini-golf	luh mee-nee-gawlf
to play	jouer	zhoo-eh
referee	l'arbitre *m*	lahr-bee-truh
shuttlecock	le volant	luh vo-lahN
single	le simple	luh saN-pluh
soccer ball	le football	luh fooht-bahl
soccer field	le terrain de football	
		luh tehr-raN duh fooht-bahl
soccer game	le match de football	
		luh mahtch duh fooht-bahl
squash	le squash	luh squash
squash ball	la balle de squash	
		lah bahl duh squash
squash racket	la raquette de squash	
		lah rah-ket duh squash
table tennis	le ping-pong	luh ping-pohN
team	l'équipe *f*	lay-keep
tennis	le tennis	luh ten-eess
tennis ball	la balle de tennis	
		lah bahl duh ten-eess
tennis racket	la raquette de tennis	
		lah rah-ket duh ten-eess
(a) tie	match nul	mahtch newl
umpire	l'arbitre *m*	lah-bee-truh
victory	la victoire	lah veek-twahr
volleyball	le volley	luh vol-lay
to win	gagner	gahn-yeh

Indoor Activities

Do you have any *playing cards / board games*?

Vous avez des *cartes à jouer / jeux de société*? voo-zah-veh day *kahrt ah zhoo-eh / zhuh duh so-see-eh-teh*

Do you play chess?

Vous jouez aux échecs? voo zhoo-eh o-zeh-shek

Is there a *sauna / gym* here?

Est-ce qu'il y a un *sauna / club de sport* ici? es-keel yah aN *so-nah / klahb duh spawr* ee-see

Do you offer *aerobics / exercise* classes as well?

Est-ce que vous proposez aussi des cours *d'aérobic / de gymnastique*? es kuh voo pro-poh-zeh o-see day koor *dah-ehr-o-beek / duh zheem-nahs-teek*

Sports

Hiking

Can you recommend an easy tour?

Vous pourriez me recommander une randonnée facile? voo poor-ee-eh muh ruh-kohN-mahN-day ewn rahN-dun-eh fah-seel

About how long will it take?

Combien de temps dure-t-elle environ? kohN-bee-aN duh tahN dewr-tel ahN-vee-rohN

Is the trail *well marked / safe for walking*?

Le chemin est bien *balisé / protégé*? luh shuh-maN eh bee-aN *bah-lee-zeh / pro-teh-zheh*

Can I go in these shoes?

Est-ce que je peux y aller avec ces chaussures? es kuh zhuh puh ee ah-lay ah-vek say sho-sewr

Sports and Leisure

Are there guided walks?	Est-ce qu'il y a des randonnées guidées? es keel yah day rahN-dun-eh ghee-day
What time's the last train?	A quelle heure descend le dernier téléphérique? ah kel uhr day-sahN luh dehrn-yeh teh-lay-feh-reek
Is this the right road for …?	Est-ce-que c'est bien la bonne route pour …? es kuh say bee-aN lah bun root poor
How far is it to …?	C'est encore loin jusqu'à …? say ahN-kaw lawn zhews-kah

Hiking: Additional Words

aerial tramway	le téléphérique luh teh-lay-feh-reek
chair lift	le télésiège luh teh-lay-see-yehzh
to climb	escalader es-kah-lah-day
climbing boots	les chaussures *f/pl* de montagne lay sho-sewr duh mohN-tahn-yuh
crampon	les crampons *m/pl* lay krahN-pohN
food	les vivres lay vee-vruh
to have a good head for heights	ne pas avoir le vertige nuh pah-zah-vwahr luh vehr-teezh
to hike	faire des randonnées fehr day rahN-dun-eh
hiking trail	le sentier de randonnée luh sahN-tyeh duh rahN-dun-eh
hut	le chalet luh shal-lay
to jog	faire du jogging fehr dew zhawg-ing
jogging	le jogging luh zhawg-ing
mountain	la montagne lah mohN-tahn-yuh
mountain climbing	l'alpinisme *m* lahl-peen-eez-muh

mountain guide	le guide de montagne
	luh gheed duh mohN-tahn-yuh
mountain rescue service	les secours *m/pl* (en montagne)
	lay suh-koor (ahN mohN tahn-yuh)
path	le chemin luh shuh-maN
ravine	les gorges *f/pl* lay gawrzh
rope	la corde la kawrd
shelter	le refuge luh ruh-fewzh
summit	le sommet luh sum-may
walkers' map	la carte de randonnée
	lah kahrt duh rahN-dun-eh
walking shoes	les chaussures *f/pl* de randonnée
	lay sho-sewr duh rahN-dun-ay
walking sticks	les cannes *f/pl* lay kahn

Bicycling

I'd like to rent a *bicycle / mountain bike*.	Je voudrais louer *un vélo / une mountain bike*. zhuh voo-dreh loo-eh *aN veh-lo / ewn moun-tain bike*
I'd like a bike with ... gears.	Je voudrais un vélo avec ... vitesses. zhuh voo-dreh aN veh-lo ah-vek ... vee-tess
Do you have a bicycle with a backpedal brake?	Avez-vous aussi un vélo avec rétropédalage? ah-veh-voo o-see aN veh-lo ah-vek ray-tro-pay-dah-lahzh
I'd like to rent it for ...	Je voudrais le louer pour ... zhuh voo-dreh luh loo-eh poor
– one day.	– une journée. ewn zhoor-nay
– two days.	– deux jours. duh zhoor
– a week.	– une semaine. ewn suh-men

Could you adjust the saddle for me?	Pourriez-vous me régler la hauteur de la selle? poor-ee-eh-voo muh ray-glay lah o-tuhr duh lah sel
Please give me a helmet as well.	Donnez-moi aussi un casque (de vélo), s'il vous plaît. dun-eh-mwah o-see aN kahsk (duh veh-lo) see voo play
Do you have a map?	Vous avez une carte? voo-zah-veh ewn kahrt

Bicycling: Additional Words

back light	le feu arrière luh fuh ah-ree-yehr
bicycle repair kit	le set de réparation pour vélo luh set duh ray-pah-rah-see-ohN poor veh-lo
bike basket	le panier porte-bagages luh pahn-yeh pawt-bah-gahzh
child seat	le siège pour enfant luh see-yehzh poor ahN-fahN
child's bicycle	le vélo pour enfant luh veh-lo poor ahN-fahN
cycling path	la piste cyclable lah peest see-klah-bluh
front light	le feu avant luh fuh ah-vahN
hand brake	le frein à main luh fraN ah maN
inner tube	la chambre à air lah shahN-bruh ah ehr
light	le feu luh fuh
pump	la pompe à air lah pohNp ah ehr
saddle	la selle lah sel
saddlebags	les sacoches f/pl lay sah-kawsh
tire	le pneu luh puh-nuh

tire pressure	la pression des pneus
	lah press-see-ohN day puh-nuh
valve	la valve lah vahlv

Adventure Sports

ballooning	le ballon luh bah-lohN
bungee jumping	le saut à l'élastique
	luh so-tah lay-lahs-teek
canoe	le canoë luh kah-noh-eh
free climbing	la varappe lah vah-rahp
glider	le planeur luh plah-nuhr
gliding	le vol à voile luh vawl ah vwahl
kayak	le kayak luh kah-yahk
paragliding	le parapente luh pah-rah-pahNt
regatta	la régate lah ray-gaht
river rafting	le rafting luh rahf-ting
row boat	le bateau à rames
	luh bah-to ah rahm
skydiving	le saut en parachute
	luh soht ahN pah-rah-shewt
thermal current	le courant ascensionnel
	luh koo-rahN-tah-sahN-see-o-nel
to ride (horseback)	faire du cheval fehr dew shuh-vahl
to sail	faire de la voile fehr duh lah vwahl

Beauty

At the Salon

| I'd like an appointment for … . | J'aimerais bien avoir rendez-vous pour … . zhem-eh-reh bee-aN ah-vwahr rahN-day-voo poor |

Qu'est-ce qu'on vous fait?

What are you having done?

I'd like …

Je voudrais … zhuh voo-dreh

– a haircut.

– me faire couper les cheveux.
muh fehr koo-pay lay shuh-vuh

– a perm.

– une permanente.
ewn pehr-mah-nahNt

– some highlights.

– le balayage luh bah-lah-yahzh

– my hair colored.

– une teinture. ewn taN-tewr

Cut, shampoo and blow-dry, please.

Une coupe, un shampooing et un brushing, s'il vous plaît. ewn koop aN shaN-pwahN eh aN bruh-shing see voo play

Just a trim, please.

Une coupe seulement, s'il vous plaît. ewn koop suhl-mahN see voo play

Que désirez-vous comme coupe?

How would you like it?

Not too short, please.

Pas trop court, s'il vous plaît.
pah tro koor see voo play

A bit shorter, please.

Un peu plus court, s'il vous plaît.
aN puh plew koor see voo play

A short crop, please.

Très court, s'il vous plaît.
treh koor see voo play

in the back

derrière dehr-yehr

in the front

devant duh-vahN

at the sides

de côté duh ko-teh

on top

en haut ahN oh

The part on the *left / right*, please.	La raie à *gauche / droite*, s'il vous plaît. lah ray ah *gosh / drwaht* see voo play
Thanks, that's fine.	Merci beaucoup, c'est très bien. mehr-see bo-koo say treh bee-aN

At the Salon: Additional Words

bangs	la frange lah frahNzh
beard	la barbe lah bahrb
black	noir nwahr
to blow-dry	faire un brushing fehr aN bruh-shing
blond	blond blohN
brown	brun braN
curls	les boucles *f/pl* (de cheveux) lay boo-kluh (duh shuh-vuh)
dandruff	les pellicules *f/pl* lay pel-ee-kewl
to dye	faire une teinture fehr ewn taN-tewr
gel	le gel luh zhel
gray	gris gree
hair	les cheveux *m/pl* lay shuh-vuh
hairspray	la laque à cheveux lah lahk ah shuh-vuh
hairstyle	la coiffure lah kwah-fewr
layers	la coupe en dégradé lah koop ahN day-grah-day
mousse	la mousse coiffante lah moos kwah-fahNt
moustache	la moustache lah moos-tahsh
shampoo	le shampooing luh shahN-pwahN
to shave	raser rah-zeh
to wash	faire un shampooing fehr aN shahN-pwahN

Beauty Treatments

I'd like a facial please.

Je voudrais un soin du visage.
zhuh voo-dreh aN swaN dew vee-sahzh

I've got …

J'ai … zhay

– normal skin.

– une peau normale.
  ewn po naw-mahl

– oily skin.
– dry skin.
– combination skin.

– une peau grasse. ewn po grahss
– une peau sèche. ewn po sehsh
– une peau mixte. ewn po meext

I have sensitive skin.

J'ai une peau sensible.
zheh ewn po sahN-see-bluh

Please use only *fragrance-free* / *hypoallergenic* products.

N'utilisez que des produits *sans parfum* / *dermatologiquement testés*, s'il vous plaît. new-tee-lee-zeh kuh day pro-dwee *sahN pahr-faN* / *dehr-mah-toh-lo-zheek-mahN tes-teh* see voo play

Could you tweeze my eyebrows?

Est-ce que vous pouvez m'épiler les sourcils? es kuh voo poo-veh may-pee-leh lay soor-see

I'd like to have my *eyelashes* / *eyebrows* dyed.

Je voudrais me faire teindre les *cils* / *sourcils*. zhuh voo-dreh muh fehr taN-druh lay *see* / *soor-see*

I'd like a half leg wax.

Je voudrais une épilation de la demi jambe, s'il vous plaît.
zhuh voo-dreh ewn eh-pee-lah-see-ohN duh lah duh-mee zhahNb see voo play

A *manicure* / *pedicure*, please.

Une *manucure* / *pédicure*, s'il vous plaît. ewn *mahn-ew-cewr* / *pay-dee-kewr* see voo play

Beauty Treatments: Additional Words

cleansing	le nettoyage luh net-wah-yahzh
face	le visage luh vee-sahzh
mask	le masque luh mahsk
moisturizing mask	le masque hydratant luh mahsk ee-drah-tahN
neck	le cou luh koo
neck and chest	le décolleté luh day-kol-teh
peeling	le peeling luh pee-ling

Well-Being

acupuncture	l'acuponcture *f* lah-kew-pohNk-tewr
massage	le massage luh mah-sahzh
mud mask	la boue lah boo
purification	l'épuration *f* lay-pew-rah-see-ohN
reflexology massage	le massage des zones de réflexe du pied luh mah-sahzh day zohn duh ray-flex dew pyeh
sauna	le sauna luh so-nah
tanning salon	le solarium luh so-lah-ree-um
yoga	le yoga luh yo-gah

Things to Do

Where's the tourist information office?
Où se trouve l'office du tourisme?

How much are the tickets?
Combien coûtent les billets?

Sightseeing

info The French Government Tourist Offices are often located in the town center (centre-ville). Their website Maison de la France (www.franceguide.com) also provides valuable information.

Tourist Information

Where's the tourist information office?	Où se trouve l'office du tourisme? oo suh troov law-feess dew toor-eez-muh
I'd like …	Je voudrais … zhuh voo-dreh
– a map of the area.	– un plan des environs. aN plahN day-zahN-vee-rohN
– a map of the town.	– un plan de la ville. aN plahN duh lah veel
– a subway map.	– un plan du métro. aN plahN dew may-troh
– an events guide.	– un calendrier des manifestations. aN kah-lahN-dree-eh day mahn-ee-fes-tah-see-ohN
Do you have a brochure in English?	Avez-vous une brochure en anglais? ah-veh-voo ewn bro-shewr ahN ahN-gleh
I'd like to visit …	J'aimerais bien visiter … zhem-eh-reh bee-aN vee-zee-teh
Are there *sightseeing tours of the town / guided walks around the town*?	Est-ce qu'il y a des *tours guidés de la ville / visites guidées de la ville*? es keel yah day *toor ghee-day duh lah veel / vee-zeet ghee-day duh lah veel*

How much is the *sightseeing tour / guided walk*?	Combien coûte *le tour guidé / la visite guidée*? kohN-bee-aN koot *luh tour ghee-day / lah vee-zeet ghee-day*
How long does the *sightseeing tour / guided walk* take?	Combien de temps dure *le tour guidé / la visite guidée*? kohN-bee-aN duh tahN dewr *luh toor ghee-day / lah vee-zeet ghee-day*
A ticket / Two tickets for the sightseeing tour, please.	*Un billet / Deux billets*, s'il vous plaît, pour le tour guidé de la ville. *aN bee-yeh / duh bee-yeh* see voo play poor luh toor ghee-day duh lah veel
What are the places of interest around here?	Qu'est-ce qu'il y a à voir ici? kes keel yah ah vwahr ee-see
One ticket / Two tickets for tomorrow's excursion to ..., please.	*Une place / Deux places* pour l'excursion de demain à ..., s'il vous plaît. *ewn plahss / duh plahss* poor lek-scewr-zee-ohN ah ... see voo play
When / Where do we meet?	*Quand / Où* est-ce que nous nous rencontrons? *kahN / oo* es kuh noo noo rahN-kohN-trohN
Do we also visit ...?	Est-ce que nous allons aussi visiter ...? es kuh noo-zahl-ohN o-see vee-zee-teh
When do we get back?	A quelle heure revenons-nous? ah kel uhr ruh-vuh-nohN noo

▶ *Accommodations, page 23;*
▶ *Asking for Directions, page 38;*
▶ *Public Transportation, page 59*

Excursions and Sights

When is ... open?	Quelles sont les heures d'ouverture de ...? kel sohN lay-zuhr doo-vehr-tewr duh
What's the admission charge?	Combien coûte l'entrée? kohN-bee-aN koot lahN-tray
How much is the tour?	Combien coûte cette excursion? kohN-bee-aN koot set ek-scewr-zee-ohN
Are there guided tours in English?	Y a-t-il des tours guidés an anglais? ee-ah-teel day toor ghee-day ahN ahN-gleh

Are there discounts for …	Est-ce qu'il y a une réduction pour … es keel yah ewn ray-dewk-see-ohN poor
– families?	– les familles? lay fah-mee
– children?	– les enfants? lay-zahN-fahN
– senior citizens?	– les personnes du troisième âge? lay pehr-sun dew trwah-zee-em ahzh
– students?	– les étudiants? lay-zeh-tew-dyahN
When does the guided tour start?	A quelle heure commence la visite? ah kel uhr kohN-mahNz lah vee-zeet
Two adults and two children, please.	Deux adultes, deux enfants, s'il vous plaît. duh-zah-dewlt duh-zahN-fahN see voo play
Are we allowed to take photographs?	Est-ce qu'on a le droit de prendre des photos? es kohN ah luh drwah duh prahN-druh day fo-toh

Excursions and Sights: Additional Words

abbey	l'abbaye f lah-bay
altar	l'autel m lo-tel
aqueduct	l'aqueduc m lah-kuh-dewk
area	la région lah ray-zhee-ohN
art	l'art m lahr
art collection	la collection de peintures lah col-ek-see-ohN duh paN-tewr
artist	l'artiste m, f lahr-teest
baroque	le baroque luh bah-rawk
bell	la cloche lah klawsh
bell tower	le clocher luh klaw-shay
botanical gardens	le jardin botanique luh zhahr-daN bo-tah-neek

brewery	la brasserie lah brahs-suh-ree
bridge	le pont luh pohN
brochure	le catalogue luh kah-tah-lawg
building	l'édifice m lay-dee-feess
bust	le buste luh bewst
capital	la capitale lah kah-pee-tahl
carving	la sculpture sur bois
	lah skewlp-tewr sewr bwah
castle	le château luh shah-toh
cathedral	la cathédrale lah kah-teh-drahl
Catholic	catholique kah-toh-leek
cave	la grotte lah grawt
ceiling	le plafond luh plah-fohN
Celtic	celtique sel-teek
cemetery	le cimetière luh seem-tyehr
ceramic	la céramique lah seh-rah-meek
chapel	la chapelle lah shah-pel
chimes	le carillon luh kah-ree-yohN
choir	le chœur luh kuhr
church	l'église f lay-gleez
church service	l'office m religieux
	law-feess ray-lee-zhyuh
church tower	le clocher luh klaw-shay
classical; ancient	antique ahN-teek
cloisters	le cloître luh klwah-truh
closed	fermé fehr-may
collection	la collection lah ko-lek-see-ohN
convent	le couvent luh koo-vahN
copy	la copie lah kaw-pee
court	la cour la coor
cross	la croix lah krwah
dome	la coupole lah koo-pohl
drawing	le dessin luh day-saN
excavations	les fouilles f/pl lay foo-yuh
exhibition	l'exposition f lex-po-zee-see-ohN

158

facade	la façade lah fah-sahd
to film	filmer feelm-eh
flea market	le marché aux puces luh mahr-shay o pewss
folk museum	le musée des arts populaires luh mew-zee day-zahr paw-pewl-lehr
forest	la forêt lah for-eh
fortress	le fort luh fawr
fountain	la fontaine lah fohN-ten
fresco	la fresque lah fresk
gallery	la galerie la gah-luh-ree
garden	le jardin luh zhahr-daN
gate	la porte lah pawrt
grave	le gothique luh go-teek
hall	la salle lah sahl
harbor	le port luh pawr
hill	la colline lah kaw-leen
house	la maison lah may-sohN
indoor market	les halles f/pl lay ahl
inscription	l'inscription f laN-screep-see-ohN
island	l'île f leel
Jewish	juif zhweef
king	le roi luh rwah
lake	le lac luh lahk
landscape	le paysage luh pay-ee-sahzh
library	la bibliothèque lah bee-blee-o-tek
marble	le marbre luh mahr-bruh
market	le marché luh mahr-shay
mausoleum	le mausolée luh mo-so-lay
memorial	le site commémoratif luh seet kohN-mem-or-ah-teef
mill	le moulin luh moo-laN
model	la maquette lah mah-ket
modern	moderne mo-dehrn
monastery	le monastère luh mohN-ah-stehr

159

monument	le monument luh mohN-ew-mahN
mosaic	la mosaïque lah mo-zah-eek
mountain	la montagne lah mohN-tahn-yuh
mountains	les montagnes *f/pl*
	lay mohN-tahn-yuh
mural	la peinture murale
	lah paN-tewr mew-rahl
museum	le musée luh mew-zeh
national park	le parc national
	luh pahrk nah-see-o-nahl
nature preserve	le site naturel protégé
	luh seet nah-tew-rel pro-teh-zheh
obelisk	l'obélisque *m* lo-bel-eesk
observatory	l'observatoire *m*
	lawb-sehr-vah-twahr
old part of town	la vieille ville lah vee-yeh veel
open	ouvert oo-vehr
opera house	l'opéra *m* lo-pehr-ah
organ	l'orgue *m* lawrg
original	l'original *m* lo-ree-zhee-nahl
painter	le peintre luh paN-truh
painting	la peinture lah paN-tewr
palace	le palais luh pah-leh
panorama	le panorama luh pah-naw-rah-mah
park	le parc luh pahrk
part of town	le quartier luh kahr-tyeh
pedestrian zone	la zone piétonne lah zohn pyeh-ton
peninsula	la péninsule lah peh-naN-sewl
picture	le tableau luh tah-blo
pillar	la colonne lah ko-lon
planetarium	le planétarium
	luh plahn-eh-tah-reeum
portal	le portail luh pawr-tigh
portrait	le portrait luh pawr-treh
pottery	la poterie lah paw-tuh-ree

160

queen	la reine lah ren
ravine	les gorges *f* lay gawrzh
relief	le relief luh ruh-lyef
religion	la religion lah reh-lee-zhee-yohN
remains	les vestiges *m/pl* lay ves-teezh
renaissance	la Renaissance lah ruh-nay-sahNs
reservoir	le lac artificiel
	luh lahk ahr-tee-fee-see-el
restored	restauré res-toh-ray
river	la rivière lah ree-vyehr
ruins	les ruines *f/pl* lay rew-een
sandstone	le grès luh greh
sculptor	le sculpteur luh skewlp-tuhr
sculpture	la sculpture lah skewlp-tewr
sights	les curiosités *f/pl*
	lay kew-ree-aws-see-teh
square	la place lah plahss
stadium	le stade luh stahd
statue	la statue lah stah-tew
style	le style luh steel
surroundings	les environs *m/pl* lay-zahN-vee-rohN
synagogue	la synagogue lah see-nah-gawg
to take photographs	prendre des photos
	pahN-druh day fo-toh
temple	le temple luh tahN-pluh
theater	le théâtre luh teh-ah-truh
to visit	visiter vee-zee-teh
tour boat	la vedette d'excursion
	lah veh-det dek-scewr-zee-ohN
tourist guide	le guide luh gheed
tourist office	le syndicat d'initiative
	luh saN-dee-kah dee-nee-see-ah-teev
tower	la tour lah toor
town	la ville lah veel
town center	le centre-ville luh sahN-truh-veel

town gate	la porte de la ville	
	lah pawt duh lah veel	
town hall	l'hôtel *m* de ville	lo-tel duh veel
town wall	les remparts *m/pl*	lay rahN-pahr
treasury	le trésor	luh treh-sawr
university	l'université *f*	lewn-ee-vehr-see-teh
valley	la vallée	lah vah-lay
vault	la voûte	lah voot
view	la vue	lah vew
wall	le mur	luh mewr
waterfall	la cascade	lah kas-kahd
window	la fenêtre	lah fen-eh-truh
works	l'œuvre *f*	luh-vruh
zoo	le zoo	luh zo

Cultural Events

What's on *this* / *next* week?	Qu'est-ce qu'il y a *cette semaine* / *la semaine prochaine* comme manifestations? kes keel yah *set suh-men* / *lah suh-men pro-shen* kohm mahn-ee-fes-tah-see-ohN
Do you have a program of events?	Est-ce que vous avez un calendrier des manifestations? es kuh voo-zah-veh aN kah-lahN-dree-yeh day mahn-ee-fes-tah-see-ohN
Where can I get tickets?	Où est-ce qu'on prend les billets? oo es kohN prahN lay bee-yeh
When does ... start?	A quelle heure commence ... ah kel uhr kohm-ahNs
– the performance	– la représentation? lah ruh-pray-sahN-tah-see-ohN
– the concert	– le concert? luh kohN-sehr
– the film	– le film? luh feelm
When do the doors open?	A quelle heure est-ce qu'on ouvre les portes? ah kel uhr es kohN oo-vruh lay pawt
Can I reserve tickets?	On peut réserver? ohN puh ray-sehr-veh
I reserved tickets under the name of ...	J'ai réservé des places au nom de ... zheh ray-sehr-veh day plahss oh nohN duh
Do you have any tickets for *today* / *tomorrow*?	Vous avez encore des billets pour *aujourd'hui* / *demain*? voo-zah-veh ahN-kaw day bee-yeh poor *o-zhoor-dwee* / *duh-maN*

163

One ticket / Two tickets for …, please.	*Un billet / Deux billets* pour …, s'il vous plaît. aN bee-yeh / duh bee-yeh poor… see voo play
– today	– aujourd'hui o-zhoor-dwee
– tonight	– ce soir suh swahr
– tomorrow	– demain duh-maN
– the … o'clock performance	– la séance de … heures lah say-ahNs duh … uhr
– the … o'clock movie	– le film de … heures luh feelm duh … uhr
How much are the tickets?	Combien coûtent les billets? kohN-bee-aN koot lay bee-yeh
Are there discounts for …	Est-ce qu'il y a une réduction pour … es keel yah ewn ray-dewk-see-ohN poor
– children?	– les enfants? lay-zahN-fahN
– senior citizens?	– les personnes du troisième âge? lay pehr-sun dew trwah-zee-em ahzh
– students?	– les étudiants? lay-zeh-tew-dyahN
I'd like to rent a pair of opera glasses.	Je voudrais louer des jumelles. zhuh voo-dreh loo-eh day zhew-mel
What time does the performance end?	À quelle heur se termine la représentation? a kel uhr suh tehr-meen lah ruh-pray-sahN-tah-see-ohN

info Local papers and weekly entertainment guides tell you what's on. In Paris, look for L'Officiel des Spectacles and Pariscope.

At the Box Office

à droite	right
à gauche	left
complet	sold out
la caisse	box office
la galerie	balcony
la location	advance booking
la loge	box
la place	seat
la place debout	standing room ticket
le balcon	circle
le deuxième balcon	rear mezzanine
le milieu	center
le parterre	orchestra (seating)
le premier balcon	front mezzanine
le rang	row

Cultural Events: Additional Words

act	l'acte *m* lahkt
actor	l'acteur *m* lahk-tuhr
actress	l'actrice *f* lahk-treess
ballet	le ballet luh bah-leh
box office	la caisse lah kess
cabaret	le cabaret luh kah-bah-reh
choir	le chœur luh kuhr
circus	le cirque luh seerk
coatroom	le vestiaire luh ves-tehr
composer	le compositeur / la compositrice luh kohN-poz-ee-tuhr / lah kohN-poz-ee-treess
conductor	le chef d'orchestre luh shef daw-kes-truh

dancer	le danseur / la danseuse
	luh dahN-suhr / lah dahN-suhz
dubbed	postsynchronisé
	pawst-saN-kro-nee-zeh
evening of traditional music and dance	la soirée folklorique
	lah swah-ray folk-law-reek
feature film	le film luh feelm
festival	le festival luh fes-tee-vahl
intermission	l'entracte *m* lahN-trahkt
movie theater	le cinéma luh see-nay-mah
music	la musique lah mew-zeek
music recital	le récital de chant
	luh ray-see-tahl duh shahN
musical	la comédie musicale
	lah ko-may-dee mew-zee-cahl
open-air theater	le théâtre de plein air
	luh teh-ah-truh duh plen air
opening night	la première lah pruhm-yehr
opera	l'opéra *m* lo-peh-rah
operetta	l'opérette *f* lo-peh-ret
orchestra	l'orchestre *m* law-kes-truh
original version	la version originale
	lah vehr-zee-ohN o-ree-zhee-nahl
play	la pièce de théâtre
	lah pee-yes duh teh-ah-truh
pop concert	le concert pop luh kohN-sehr pawp
program	le programme luh pro-grahm
rock concert	le concert rock luh kohN-sehr rawk
seat	la place lah plahss
singer	le chanteur / la chanteuse
	luh shahN-tuhr / lah shahN-tuhz
subtitle	les sous-titres *m/pl*
	lay soo-tee-truh
theater	le théâtre luh teh-ah-truh
variety show	les variétés *f/pl* lay vah-ree-eh-teh

Nightlife

What's there to do here in the evening?	Où est-ce qu'on peut sortir le soir par ici? oo es kohN puh saw-teer luh swahr pahr ee-see
Where can you go dancing around here?	Où est-ce qu'on peut aller danser par ici? oo es kohN puh ah-lay dahN-say pahr ee-see
Is it for *young* / *older* people?	On y rencontre plutôt *des jeunes* / *des adultes*? ohN-ee rahN-kohN-truh plew-toh *day zhuhn* / *day-zah-dewlt*
Is evening attire required?	Il faut se mettre en tenue de soirée? ee fo suh met-truh ahN ten-ew duh swah-ray
Is this seat taken?	Est-ce que cette place est prise? es kuh set plahss eh pree-zuh
Do you serve refreshments here?	Est-ce qu'on peut manger quelque chose ici? es kohN puh mahN-zheh kel-kuh shoze ee-see
Could I see the wine list?	Est-ce que vous avez la carte des vins? es kuh voo-zah-veh lah cahrt day vaN

▶ *Eating and Drinking, page 77*

What would you like to drink?	Qu'est-ce que vous voulez boire? kes-kuh voo voo-lay bwahr
A glass of wine, please.	Un verre de vin, s'il vous plaît. aN vehr duh vaN see voo play

▶ *Asking Someone Out, page 17;*
▶ *Flirting and Romance, page 18*

| Would you like to dance? | Je peux vous inviter pour cette danse? zhuh puh voo-zahN-vee-teh poor set dahNs |
| You dance very well. | Vous dansez très bien. voo-dahNs-eh treh bee-aN |

Nightlife: Additional Words

band	le groupe luh group
bar	le bar luh bahr
casino	le casino luh kah-zee-no
cocktail	le cocktail luh kawk-tail
dance	la soirée dansante lah swah-ray dahN-sahNt
drink	la boisson lah bwah-sohN
loud	bruyant brew-yahN

Money,
Mail and
Police

POSTES

HEURES
DES LEVÉES

DU LUNDI
AU VENDREDI
8H30

PAS DE LEVEE
LE SAMEDI

PLACE ARISTIDE
BRIAND 84210

LA POSTE
PERNES

I'd like to cash a traveler's check.
Je voudrais encaisser un chèque de voyage.

Is there any mail for me?
Vous avez du courrier pour moi?

Money Matters

info The currency in France and Belgium is the euro, divided into 100 cents (centimes); the currency in Switzerland is the Swiss franc. Not all banks provide exchange services. Hotels sometimes do but only to their guests. Cash can also be obtained from ATMs with credit and ATM cards. Instructions are sometimes in English.

Excuse me, where's there a bank around here?	Pardon, vous pourriez m'indiquer une banque dans le coin? pahr-dohN voo poo-ree-eh maN-dee-keh ewn bahNk dahN luh kwaN
Where can I exchange some money?	Où est-ce que je peux changer de l'argent? oo es kuh zhuh puh shahNzh-eh duh lahr-zhahN
I'd like to change *dollars / pounds.*	Je voudrais changer des *dollars / livres.* zhuh voo-dreh shahNzh-eh day *dol-lahr / leev-ruh*
I'd like to cash a traveler's check.	Je voudrais encaisser un chèque de voyage. zhuh voo-dreh ahN-kess-eh aN shek duh vwah-yahzh
Votre passeport, s'il vous plaît.	Your passport, please.
Une signature ici, s'il vous plaît.	Sign here, please.
En quelle coupure voulez-vous votre argent?	How would you like it?

In small bills, please.	Donnez-moi des petites coupures, s'il vous plaît. dun-eh-mwah day puh-teet koo-pewr see voo play
Please give me some change as well.	Donnez-moi aussi un peu de monnaie. dun-eh-mwah o-see aN puh duh muh-nay

▶ *Numbers, see inside front cover*

Money Matters: Additional Words

amount	le montant luh mohN-tahN
automatic teller machine (ATM)	le distributeur de billets luh dee-stree-bew-tuhr duh bee-yeh
card number	le numéro de la carte luh new-may-ro duh lah kahrt
cash transfer	le virement (bancaire) luh veer-mahN (bahN-kehr)
check	le chèque luh shehk
coin	la pièce lay pee-yes
counter	la caisse lah kess
counter	le guichet luh ghee-shay
credit card	la carte de crédit lah kahrt duh kray-dee
currency	la valeur lah vah-luhr
currency exchange	le bureau de change luh bew-ro duh shahNzh
exchange rate	le cours luh koor
money	l'argent *m* lahr-zhahN
PIN	le code secret luh code suh-kreh
savings bank	la caisse d'épargne lah kess day-pahr-nyuh
signature	la signature lah seen-yah-tewr
transfer	le virement luh veer-mahN

Post Office

Where's the nearest
post office / mailbox?

Où est la *poste / boîte aux lettres* la
plus proche? oo eh lah *pawst / bwaht
ah let-truh* lah plew prawsh

How much is a *letter /
postcard* to ...

Combien coûte une *lettre / carte*
pour ... kohN-bee-aN koot ewn *let-
truh / kahrt* poor

A ...-cent stamp,
please.

Un timbre à ... centimes, s'il vous
plaît. aN taN-bruh ah ... sahN-team see
voo play

I'd like to send this
letter ..., please.

Cette lettre ..., s'il vous plaît.
set let-truh ... see voo play

– by airmail
– special delivery
– by regular mail

– par avion pahr ahv-yohN
– par exprès pahr ex-press
– par voie maritime
   pahr vwah mah-ree-teem

I'd like to send this
package.

Je voudrais poster ce colis.
zhuh voo-dreh paws-teh suh ko-lee

Is there any mail for
me?

Vous avez du courrier pour moi?
voo-zah-veh dew koor-ee-eh poor
mwah

Post Office: Additional Words

address   l'adresse *f* lah-dress
addressee   le destinataire luh des-tee-nah-tehr
declaration of value la valeur déclarée
                         lah vah-luhr day-klah-ray
express letter   la lettre exprès lah let-truh ex-press

insured package	le colis à valeur déclarée
	luh ko-lee ah vah-luhr day-klah-ray
postcard	la carte postale lah kahrt paws-tahl
to send	envoyer ahN-vwah-yeh
small package	le paquet luh pah-keh
special stamp	le timbre spécial
	luh taN-bruh spay-see-ahl
stamp	le timbre(-poste) luh taN-bruh (pawst)
zip code	le code postal luh code paws-tahl

Police

Where's the nearest police station?	Où est le poste de police le plus proche? oo eh luh pawst duh po-leess luh plew prawsh
I'd like to report …	Je voudrais dénoncer … zhuh voo-dreh day-nohN-say
– a theft.	– un vol. aN vawl
– a mugging.	– une agression. ewn ah-gres-see-ohN
– a rape.	– un viol. aN vee-awl

▶ *Accidents, page 52*

My … has been stolen.	On m'a volé ♂ mon / ♀ ma … ohN mah-vaw-lay ♂ *mohN* / ♀ *mah*
I've lost …	J'ai perdu … zheh pehr-dew
My car's been broken into.	On a ouvert ma voiture par effraction. ohN-ah oo-vehr mah vwah-tewr pahr eh-frahk-see-ohN
I've been *cheated* / *beaten up*.	On m'a *dupé* / *agressé*. ohN mah *dew-pay* / *ah-gres-say*

173

I need a report for insurance purposes.	J'ai besoin d'une attestation pour mon assurance. zheh buh-zwaN dewn ah-tes-tah-see-oN poor mohN ah-sewr-rahNs
I'd like to speak to my *lawyer / consulate*.	Je voudrais parler à *mon avocat / avec mon consulat*. zhuh voo-dreh pahr-lay ah mohN ah-vo-kah / ah-vek mohN kohN-sew-lah
I'm innocent.	Je suis innocent. zhuh swee een-no-sahN
Vos papiers, s'il vous plaît.	Your identification, please.
Adressez-vous à votre consulat.	Please contact your consulate.

Police: Additional Words

accident	l'accident m lahk-see-dahN
car radio	l'autoradio m lo-toh-rah-dee-oh
counterfeit money	la fausse monnaie lah fohss mun-ay
handbag	le sac à main luh sahk ah maN
lost and found	le bureau des objets trouvés luh bew-ro day-zawb-zheh troo-veh
narcotics	la drogue lah drawg
pickpocket	le pickpocket luh peek-paw-ket
police	la police lah po-leess
policeman	le gendarme luh gahN-dahrm
stolen	volé vaw-lay
thief	le voleur luh vol-uhr
wallet	le portefeuille luh pawt-fuh-yuh
witness	le témoin luh teh-mwaN

Health

Where's the nearest pharmacy?
Où est la pharmacie la plus proche?

Please call an ambulance!
Appelez une ambulance s'il vous plaît!

Pharmacy

Where's the nearest pharmacy?	Où est la pharmacie la plus proche? oo eh lah fahr-mah-see lah plew prawsh
Do you have anything for …?	Vous avez quelque chose contre …? voo-zah-veh kel-kuh shoze kohN-truh

▶ *Illnesses and Complaints, page 186*

I need this medicine.	J'ai besoin de ce médicament. zheh buh-zwaN duh suh may-dee-kah-mahN
A small pack will do.	Une petite boîte suffira. ewn puh-teet bwaht sew-fee-rah
Ce médicament est uniquement délivré sur ordonnance.	You need a prescription for this medicine.
Nous ne l'avons pas en magasin.	I'm afraid we don't have that.
Nous devons le commander.	We'll have to order it.
When can I pick it up?	Vous l'aurez quand? voo loh-ray kahN
How should I take it?	Comment est-ce que je dois le prendre? kohN-mahN es kuh zhuh dwah luh prahN-druh

Medication Information

ingredients	composition
applications	indications thérapeutiques
contraindications	contre-indications

dosage instructions	posologie
infants	enfants
children (over/under ... years)	enfants (à partir de / jusqu'à ... ans)
pregnant women	femmes enceintes
adults	adultes
three times a day	trois fois par jour
one tablet / one caplet	un comprimé
ten drops	dix gouttes
one teaspoon	une cuillère à café
to be taken as directed	conformément aux prescriptions du médecin

directions	mode d'administration
dissolve on the tongue	laisser fondre dans la bouche
after meals	après les repas
before meals	avant les repas
on an empty stomach	à jeun
to be swallowed whole, unchewed	avaler sans croquer

application	indications (thérapeutiques)
external	externe
rectal	rectal
internal	interne
oral	oral

side effects	effets secondaires
may cause drowsiness	peut provoquer une somnolence
you are advised not to drive	peut provoquer des troubles de la vigilance sur la route

Medicine and Medications

adhesive bandage	le pansement luh pahNs-mahN
after sunburn lotion	la pommade contre les coups de soleil lah pum-ahd kohN-truh lay koo duh so-lay
anti-itch cream	la pommade contre les démangeaisons lah pum-ahd kohN-truh lay day-mahN-zheh-zohN
antibiotic	l'antibiotique *m* lahN-tee-bee-o-teek
antiseptic	le désinfectant luh day-saN-fek-tahN
antiseptic ointment	la pommade cicatrisante lah pum-ahd see-kah-tree-sahNt
birth control pill	la pilule contraceptive lah pee-lewl kohN-trah-sep-teev
circulatory stimulant	le médicament pour la circulation du sang luh may-dee-kah-mahN poor lah seer-kew-lah-see-ohN dew sahN
condoms	les préservatifs *m/pl* lay pray-sehr-vah-teev
cough medicine	le sirop contre la toux luh see-ro kohN-truh lah too
drops	les gouttes *f/pl* lay goot
ear drops	les gouttes *f/pl* pour les oreilles lay goot poor lay-zo-ray
elastic bandage	la bande élastique lah bahNd eh-lahs-teek
eye drops	le collyre luh kawl-leer
first-aid kit	les pansements *m/pl* lay pahNs-mahN
gauze bandage	la bande de gaze lah bahNd duh gahz

headache pills	les comprimés *m/pl* contre le mal de tête lay kohN-pree-may kohN-truh luh mahl duh tet
homeopathic	homéopathique o-may-o-pah-teek
indigestion tablets	les comprimés *m/pl* contre les maux d'estomac lay kohN-pree-may kohN-truh lay moh day-sto-mah
injection	la piqûre lah pee-kewr
insulin	l'insuline *f* laN-sew-leen
iodine	l'iode *m* lee-awd
laxative	le laxatif luh lahx-ah-teef
nose drops	les gouttes *f/pl* pour le nez lay goot poor luh nay
ointment for a sun allergy	la pommade (contre les allergies au soleil) lah pum-ahd (kohN-truh lay-zah-lehr-zhee o so-lay)
ointment for mosquito bites	la pommade contre les piqûres de moustiques lah pum-ahd kohN-truh lay pee-kewr duh moo-steek
painkiller	l'analgésique *m* lahn-ahl-zheh-seek
powder	la poudre lah poo-druh
prescription	l'ordonnance *f* law-dun-ahNs
sleeping pills	les somnifères *m/pl* lay sum-nee-fehr
something for …	le remède contre … luh ruh-may-dee kohN-truh
suppository	le suppositoire luh sew-paw-zee-twahr
tablets	les comprimés lay kohN-pree-may
thermometer	le thermomètre luh tehr-mo-meh-truh
throat drops	les cachets *m/pl* pour la gorge lay kah-shay poor luh gawrzh
tranquilizer	le calmant luh kahl-mahN

► *Illnesses and Complaints, page 186*

Looking for a Doctor

Can you recommend a *doctor* / *dentist*?
Est-ce que vous pouvez me recommander un *médecin généraliste* / *dentiste*? es kuh voo poo-veh muh ruh-kohN-mahN-day aN *made-saN zhen-eh-rah-leest* / *dahN-teest*

Does *he* / *she* speak English?
Parle-t-*il* / *elle* anglais? pahrl-uh-*teel* / *tel* ahN-gleh

Where's *his* / *her* office?
Où est son cabinet? oo eh sohN kah-bee-nay

Can *he* / *she* come to see me?
Est-ce qu'il / *Est-ce qu'elle* pourrait venir me voir? es *keel* / *es-kel* poo-reh ven-eer muh vwahr

info You'll be expected to pay doctors and dentists on the spot. Make sure your health insurance covers you while abroad.

Please call *an ambulance* / *a doctor*!
Appelez *une ambulance* / *le S.A.M.U.*, s'il vous plaît. ah-play *ewn ahN-bew-lahNs* / *luh ess ah em ew* see voo play

My *husband* / *wife* is sick.
Mon mari / *Ma femme* est malade. *mohN-mah-ree* / *mah fahm* eh mah-lahd

Physicians

dentist	le dentiste luh dahN-teest
dermatologist	le dermatologue luh dehr-mah-toh-lawg
doctor	le médecin luh made-saN

ear, nose and throat doctor	l'oto-rhino-laryngologiste *m* lo-toh-ree-no-lah-raN-go-lo-zheest
eye specialist	l'oculiste *m* loh-kew-leest
female doctor	le médecin luh made-saN
female gynecologist	la gynécologue lah zheen-eh-kaw-lawg
gynecologist	le gynécologue luh zheen-eh-kaw-lawg
homeopathic doctor	le practicien de médecines parallèles luh prahk-tee-see-ahN duh made-seen pah-rah-lel
internist	le spécialiste des maladies internes luh spay-see-ah-leest day mah-lah-dee aN-tehrn
orthopedist	l'orthopédiste *m* lor-toh-pay-deest
pediatrician	le pédiatre luh pay-dee-ah-truh
physician	le médecin généraliste luh made-saN zhehn-nehr-ah-leest
urologist	l'urologue *m* lew-ro-lawg
veterinarian	le vétérinaire luh veh-teh-ree-nehr

▶ *At the Dentist's, page 191*

At the Doctor's Office

I've got a (bad) cold.	J'ai un (gros) rhume. zheh aN (gro) rewm
I've got …	J'ai … zheh
– a headache.	– mal à la tête. mahl ah lah tet
– a sore throat.	– mal à la gorge. mahl ah lah gawrzh
– a high temperature.	– de la fièvre. duh lah fee-ev-ruh
– the flu.	– la grippe. lah greep
– diarrhea.	– la diarrhée. lah dee ah-ray
I don't feel well.	Je ne me sens pas bien. zhuh muh sahN pah bee-aN
I'm dizzy.	J'ai des vertiges. zheh day vehr-teezh
My … *hurts / hurt*.	J'ai mal *à / aux* … zheh mahl *ah / o*

▶ *Body Parts and Organs, page 184*

It hurts here.	J'ai mal ici. zheh mahl ee-see

Emergency calls:
SAMU (medical emergencies): 15
Police emergencies: 17
Fire emergencies: 18

I've vomited (several times).	J'ai vomi (plusieurs fois). zheh voh-mee (pluh-zee-uhr fwah)
I've got an upset stomach.	J'ai l'estomac barbouillé. zheh les-toh-mah bahr-boo-yeh
I fainted.	J'ai perdu connaissance. zheh pehr-dew kohN-nay-sahNs

I can't move my …	Je ne peux pas bouger ♂ *mon* / ♀ *ma*… zhuh nuh pew pah boo-zhay ♂ *moN* / ♀ *mah*
I've hurt myself.	Je me suis blessé. zhuh muh swee bles-say
I fell.	Je suis tombé. zhuh swee tohN-bay
I've been *stung* / *bitten* by …	J'ai été *piqué* / *mordu* par … zheh eh-teh *pee-keh* / *maw-dew* pahr
I'm allergic to penicillin.	Je suis allergique à la pénicilline. zhuh swee-zah-lehr-zheek ah lah pen-ee-see-leen
I've got *high* / *low* blood pressure.	Je souffre d'*hypertension* / *hypotension*. zhuh soo-fruh *dee-pehr-tahN-see-ohN* / *dee-po-tahN-see-ohN*
I've got a pacemaker.	Je porte un pacemaker. zhuh pawrt aN pace-may-kehr
I'm (… months) pregnant.	Je suis enceinte (de … mois). zhuh swee-zaN-saNt (duh… mwah)
I'm diabetic.	Je suis diabétique. zhuh swee dee-ah-bay-teek
Où avez-vous mal?	Where's the pain?
Ça vous fait mal ici?	Does it hurt here?
Ouvrez la bouche.	Open your mouth.
Montrez la langue.	Show me your tongue.
Enlevez le haut, s'il vous plaît.	Undress to the waist, please.
Nous devons vous faire une radio.	We'll have to X-ray you.

Inspirez profondément. Ne respirez plus.	Take a deep breath. Hold your breath.
Depuis quand avez-vous ces problèmes?	How long have you had this problem?
J'ordonne une prise *de sang* / *d'urine*.	I'll need a *blood* / *urine* sample.
Il faut vous opérer.	You'll have to have an operation.
Ce n'est rien de grave.	It's nothing serious.
Revenez *demain* / *dans … jours*.	Come back *tomorrow* / *in … days*.
Can you give me a doctor's note?	Est-ce que vous pourriez me faire un certificat? es kuh voo poor-ee-eh muh fehr aN sehr-tee-fee-kah
Do I have to come back?	Est-ce que je dois revenir? es kuh zhuh dwah ruh-ven-eer
Could you give me a receipt for my medical insurance?	Pourriez-vous me donner une facture pour mon assurance, s'il vous plaît? poor-ee-eh voo muh dun-eh ewn fahk-tewr poor mohN-nah-sewr-ahNs see voo play

Body Parts and Organs

abdomen	le ventre luh vahN-truh
ankle	la cheville lah shuh-vee
appendix	l'appendice *m* lah-pahN-dees
arm	le bras luh brah
back	le dos luh doh

bladder	la vessie lah ves-see
blood	le sang luh sahN
body	le corps luh kawr
bone	l'os *m* loss
bottom	le séant luh say-ahN
brain	le cerveau luh sehr-vo
bronchial tubes	les bronches *f/pl* lay brohNsh
calf	le mollet luh maw-leh
chest	la poitrine lah pwah-treen
collarbone	la clavicule lah klah-vee-kewl
disc	le disque intervertébral
	luh deesk aN-tehr-vehr-teh-brahl
ear	l'oreille *f* lo-ray
eye	l'œil *m* les yeux *pl* luh-yuh lay-zyuh
face	le visage luh vee-zahzh
finger	le doigt luh dwah
foot	le pied luh pee-eh
forehead	le front luh frohN
frontal sinus	le sinus frontal
	luh see-newss frohN-tahl
gall bladder	la bile lah beel
genitals	les organes *m/pl* génitaux
	lay-zor-gahn zheh-nee-toh
hand	la main lah maN
head	la tête lah tet
heart	le cœur luh kuhr
heel	le talon luh tah-lohN
hip	la hanche lah ahNsh
intestine	les intestins *m/pl* lay-zaN-tes-taN
joint	l'articulation *f*
	lahr-tee-kew-lah-see-ohN
kidney	le rein luh raN
knee	le genou luh zhen-oo
kneecap	la rotule lah ro-tewl
leg	la jambe lah zhahNb

liver	le foie luh fwah
lungs	les poumons *m/pl* lay poo-mohN
mouth	la bouche lah boosh
mucus membrane	la muqueuse lah mew-kuhz
muscle	le muscle luh mews-kluh
neck	le cou luh koo
neck	la nuque lah newk
nerve	le nerf luh nehr
nose	le nez luh nay
pelvis	le bassin luh bah-saN
rib	la côte lah kawt
shinbone	le tibia luh tee-bee-ah
shoulder	l'épaule *f* lay-pohl
sinus	le sinus luh see-newss
skin	la peau lah po
spine	la colonne vertébrale lah kol-un vehr-teh-brahl
stomach	l'estomac *m* less-toh-mah
tendon	le tendon luh than-dohN
throat	la gorge lah gawrzh
thyroid gland	la thyroïde lah teer-aw-eed
toe	l'orteil *m* lor-teh
tongue	la langue lah lahNg
tonsils	les amygdales *f/pl* lay-zah-mee-dahl
tooth	la dent lah dahN
vertebrae	la vertèbre lah vehr-teb-ruh

Illnesses and Complaints

abscess	l'abcès *m* lahb-seh
AIDS	le sida luh see-dah
allergy	l'allergie *f* lahl-ehr-zhee
angina	l'angine *f* lahN-zheen

appendicitis	l'appendicite *f* lah-pahN-dee-seet
asthma	l'asthme *m* lahsm
bite	la morsure lah mawr-sewr
bite, sting	la piqûre lah pee-kewr
blister	la vessie lah ves-see
breathing problems	les difficultés à respirer
	lay dee-fee-kewl-teh ah res-pee-ray
broken	cassé kah-say
bronchitis	la bronchite lah brawn-sheet
bruise	la contusion lah kohN-tew-zee-ohN
burn	la brûlure lah brew-lewr
bypass	le by-pass luh by-pass
cancer	le cancer luh kahN-sehr
cardiac infarction	l'infarctus *m* laN-fahrk-tewss
chicken pox	la varicelle lah vah-ree-sel
chills	les frissons *m/pl* lay frees-sohN
circulatory problems	les troubles *m/pl* circulatoires
	lay troo-bluh seer-kew-lah-twahr
cold	le rhume luh rewm
colic	la colique lah kaw-leek
concussion	la commotion cérébrale
	lah koh-mo-see-ohN say-ray-brahl
conjunctivitis	la conjonctivite
	lah kohN-zhohNd-tee-veet
constipation	la constipation
	lah kohN-stee-pah-see-ohN
cough	la toux lah too
cramp	la crampe lah krahNp
cystitis	la cystite lah sees-teet
diabetes	le diabète luh dee-ah-bet
diarrhea	la diarrhée lah dee-ah-ray
disease	la maladie lah mah-lah dee
dislocated	luxé lewx-eh
dizziness	les vertiges *m/pl* lay vehr-teezh
fever	la fièvre lah fee-ev-ruh

flu	**la grippe** lah greep
food poisoning	**l'intoxication** f **alimentaire** laN-tawx-ee-kah-see-ohN ah-lee-mahN-tehr
fungal infection	**la mycose** lah mee-kawz
heart attack	**la crise cardiaque** lah kreez kahr-dee-ahk
heart problem	**l'anomalie** f **cardiaque** lahn-o-mah-lee kahr-dee-ahk
heartburn	**les brûlures** f/pl **(d'estomac)** lay brew-lewr (day-stoh-mah)
hemorrhoids	**les hémorroïdes** f/pl lay em-or-ro-eed
hernia	**la hernie** lah ehr-nee
herpes	**l'herpès** m lehr-pez
high blood pressure	**la haute tension** lah oht tahn-see-ohN
infection	**l'infection** f laN-fek-see-ohN
infectious	**contagieux** kohN-tah-zhee-uh
inflammation	**l'inflammation** f laN-flah-mah-see-ohN
injury	**la blessure** lah bles-sewr
kidney stones	**les calculs** m/pl **rénaux** lay kahl-kewl ray-noh
low blood pressure	**la basse tension** lah bahss tahn-see-ohN
lower back pain	**le lumbago** luh laN-bah-goh
malaria	**la malaria** lah mahl-ah-ree-ah
meningitis	**la méningite** lah may-nahN-geet
migraine	**la migraine** lah mee-gren
motion sickness	**le mal des voyages** luh mahl day vwah-ahzh
nausea	**le mal au cœur** luh mahl o kuhr
neuralgia	**la névralgie** lah nev-rahl-zhee

nose bleed	les saignements *m/pl* de nez
	lay sen-yuh-mahN duh nay
pacemaker	le pacemaker luh pace-make-ehr
periods	les menstruations *f/pl*
	lay mahN-strew-ah-see-ohN
pneumonia	la pneumonie lah pnuh-mun-ee
polio	la poliomyélite
	lah paw-lee-um-yeh-leet
pulled ligament	l'entorse *f* lahN-tors
pulled muscle	le claquage musculaire
	luh klah-kahzh mews-kew-lehr
pulled tendon	l'élongation *f* lay-lohN-gah-see-ohN
rash	l'éruption *f* cutanée
	lay-rewp-see-ohN kew-tahn-eh
rheumatism	le rhumatisme luh ree-mah-teez-muh
sciatica	la sciatique lah syah-teek
sexually transmitted	la maladie vénérienne
disease (STD)	lah mah-lah-dee veh-nay-ree-en
shock	le choc luh shawk
sprained	foulé foo-lay
sting	la piqûre lah pee-kewr
stomach ache	les maux *m/pl* d'estomac
	les mo day-stoh-mah
stomach ulcer	l'ulcère *m* à l'estomac
	lewl-sehr ah les-toh-mah
stroke	l'attaque *f* (d'apoplexie)
	lah-tahk (dah-po-plex-ee)
sunburn	le coup de soleil luh koo duh so-lay
sunstroke	l'insolation *f* laN-so-lah-see-ohN
swelling	l'enflure *f* lahn-flewr
tick bite	la piqûre de tique
	lah pee-kewr duh teek
tonsillitis	l'amygdalite *f* lah-mee-dah-leet
torn ligament	la déchirure des ligaments
	lah day-she-rewr day lee-gah-mahN

ulcer	l'ulcère lewl-sehr
vomiting	les vomissements *m/pl*
	lay vaw-meess-mahN
whooping cough	la coqueluche lah kaw-kel-ewsh
wound	la blessure lah bles-sewr

At the Hospital

| Is there anyone here who can speak English? | Est-ce qu'il y a quelqu'un qui parle anglais? es keel yah kel-kaN kee pahrl ahN-gleh |

▶ *At the Doctor's Office, page 182*

| I'd rather have the operation in the US. | Je préfère me faire opérer aux États-Unis. zhuh pray-fehr muh fair o-pay-ray oh-zeh-tahs-ew-nee |

| I'm insured for repatriation expenses. | Mon assurance couvre les frais de rapatriement. mohN ah-sew-rahNs koov-ruh lay freh duh rah-pah-tree mahN |

| Please let my family know. | Prévenez ma famille, s'il vous plaît. pray-vuh-nay mah fah-mee see voo play |

| Nurse, could you help me, please? | ♂ Infirmier / ♀ Infirmière, pouvez-vous m'aider, s'il vous plaît? aN-feerm-yehr / aN-feerm-yeh poo-veh-voo med-eh see voo play |

| Please give me *a painkiller / sleeping pill*. | Donnez-moi quelque chose *contre la douleur / pour dormir*, s'il vous plaît. dun-ay mwah kel-kuh-shoze *kohN-truh lah doo-luhr / poor dawr-meer* see voo play |

At the Dentist's

This tooth hurts.	J'ai mal à cette dent. zheh mahl ah set dahN
This tooth is broken.	La dent s'est cassée. lah dahN seh kah-say
I've lost *a filling* / *a crown*.	J'ai perdu *un plombage* / *une couronne*. zheh pehr-dew aN *plohN-bahzh* / *ewn koor-un*
Could you do a temporary job on the tooth?	Est-ce que vous pourriez soigner la dent de façon provisoire? es kuh voo poor-ee-eh swan-yeh lah dahN duh fah-sohN pro-vee-swahr
Please don't pull the tooth.	S'il vous plaît, ne m'arrachez pas la dent. see voo play nuh mah-rah-sheh pah lah dahN
Give me an injection, please.	Faites-moi une injection, s'il vous plaît. fet-mwah ewn aN-zhek-see-ohN see voo play
Can you repair these dentures?	Pourriez-vous réparer cette prothèse? poor-ee-eh-voo ray-pah-ray set praw-tehz
Vous avez besoin …	You need …
– d'un bridge.	– a bridge.
– d'un plombage.	– a filling.
– d'une couronne.	– a crown.
Je dois extraire la dent.	I'll have to take the tooth out.
Rincez bien.	Rinse well.

Ne rien manger pendant deux heures.	Don't eat anything for two hours.

At the Dentist's: Additional Words

amalgam filling	l'amalgame *m* lah-mahl-gahm
braces	l'appareil *m* dentaire lah-pah-ray dahN-tehr
cavity	la carie lah kah-ree
composite filling	le composite luh kohN-po-zeet
dentures	le dentier luh dahN-tee-eh
gold filling	le plombage en or luh plohN-bahzh ahN-awr
gum infection	l'inflammation *f* de la gencive laN-flah-mah-see-ohN duh lah zhahN-seev
gums	la gencive lah zhahN-seev
impression	l'empreinte *f* lahN-praNt
inlay	l'inlay *m* leen-lay
jaw	la mâchoire lah mah-shwahr
nerve	le nerf luh nehr
periodontal disease	la parodontose lah pah-rah-dohN-toh-zuh
porcelain filling	le plombage en porcelaine luh plohN-bahzh ahN pawr-suh-len
root	la racine lah rah-seen
root canal	le traitement de la racine lah tret-mahN duh lah rah-seen
tartar	le tartre luh tahr-truh
temporary filling	le traitement provisoire luh tret-mahN pro-vee-zwahr
tooth	la dent lah dahN
wisdom tooth	la dent de sagesse lah dahN duh sah-zhess

Time and the Calendar

What time is it?
Quelle heure est-il?

It's one o'clock.
Il est une heure.

Time of the Day

What time is it?	Quelle heure est-il? kel uhr eh-teel
It's one o'clock.	Il est une heure. eel eh ewn uhr
It's two o'clock.	Il est deux heures. eel eh duh-zuhr
It's *noon / midnight*.	Il est *midi / minuit*. eel eh *mee-dee / meen-wee*
It's five after four.	Il est quatre heures cinq. eel eh kaht-ruhr saNk
It's a quarter after five.	Il est cinq heures et quart. eel eh saNk uhr eh kahr
It's 6:30.	Il est six heures et demie. eel eh see-zuhr eh duh-mee
It's twenty-five to four.	Il est quinze heures trente-cinq. eel eh kaNz-uhr trahNt-saNk

info In general, the 24-hour clock is used in France. This means, rather than saying, "It's 2:30", it is better to say "It's 14:30." (Il est quartorze heures et demi.)

It's a quarter to nine.	Il est neuf heures moins le quart. eel eh nuhv-uhr mwaN luh kahr
It's ten to eight.	Il est huit heures moins dix. eel eh weet uhr mwaN deess
At what time?	A quelle heure? ah kel uhr
At ten o'clock.	A dix heures. ah dee-zuhr
Until eleven (o'clock).	Jusqu'à onze heures. zhews-kah ohNz uhr

Time and the Calendar

From eight till nine.	De huit heures à neuf heures. duh weet-uhr ah nuhv-uhr
Between ten and twelve.	Entre dix et douze. ahN-truh deess eh dooz
In half an hour.	Dans une demi-heure. dahN-sewn duh-mee uhr
It's (too) late.	Il est (trop) tard. eel eh (tro) tahr
It's too early.	Il est encore trop tôt. eel eh ahN-kawr tro toe

► *Numbers, see inside front cover*

Time Expressions: Additional Words

15 minutes	le quart d'heure luh kahr-duhr
a month ago	il y a un mois eel yah aN mwah
afternoon	l'après-midi *m* lah-preh-mee-dee
at around noon	à midi ah mee-dee
at dawn	à l'aube ah lobe
at night	la nuit la nwee
day	le jour luh zhoor
early	tôt toe
evening	le soir luh swahr
for	pour poor
half an hour	la demi-heure lah duh-mee-uhr
hour	l'heure *f* luhr
in the afternoon	l'après-midi *m* lah-preh-mee-dee
in the evening	le soir luh swahr
in the morning	le matin luh mah-taN
in two weeks	dans quinze jours dahN kaNz zhoor
late	tard tahr
later	plus tard plew tahr
minute	la minute lah meen-ewt

month	le mois luh mwah
morning	le matin luh mah-taN
next year	l'année *f* prochaine
	lah-nay pro-shen
night	la nuit lah nwee
now	maintenant maN-tuh-nahN
recently	il y a peu de temps
	eel yah puh duh tahN
second	la seconde lah suh-kohNd
since	depuis duh-pwee
sometimes	quelquefois kel-kuh-fwah
soon	bientôt bee-aN-toe
the day after tomorrow	après-demain ah-preh-duh-maN
the day before	avant-hier ah-vahN-tyehr
yesterday	
this afternoon	cet après-midi set ah-preh-mee-dee
this morning	ce matin suh mah-taN
time	le temps luh tahN
today	aujourd'hui oh-zhoor-dwee
tomorrow	demain duh-maN
tonight	ce soir suh swahr
until	jusqu'à zhews-kah
week	la semaine lah suh-men
year	l'année *f* lah-nay
yesterday	hier yehr

Seasons

spring	le printemps luh praN-tahN
summer	l'été *m* lay-teh
autumn	l'automne *m* lo-tun
winter	l'hiver *m* lee-vehr

Time and the Calendar

Date

What's today's date?	On est le combien aujourd'hui? ohN es luh kohN-bee-aN oh-zhoor-dwee
Today's July 2nd.	Aujourd'hui, on est le deux juillet. oh-zhoor-dwee ohN-eh luh duh zhwee-eh
On the 4th of *this* / *next* month.	Le quatre *de ce mois* / *du mois prochain*. luh kah-truh *duh suh mwah* / *dew mwah pro-shaN*
Until March 10th.	Jusqu'au dix mars. zhews-koh dee mahrss
We're leaving on August 20th.	Nous partons le vingt août. noo pahr-tohN luh vaN oot

Days of the Week

Monday	lundi laN-dee
Tuesday	mardi mahr-dee
Wednesday	mercredi mehr-kruh-dee
Thursday	jeudi zhuh-dee
Friday	vendredi vahN-druh-dee
Saturday	samedi sahm-dee
Sunday	dimanche dee-mahNsh

Months

January	janvier zhahN-vee-eh
February	février feh-vree-eh
March	mars mahrss
April	avril ah-vreel
May	mai meh

June	juin zhwaN
July	juillet zhwee-eh
August	août oot
September	septembre sep-tahN-bruh
October	octobre aw-tawb-ruh
November	novembre no-vahN-bruh
December	décembre day-sahN-bruh

Holidays

All Saints' Day	la Toussaint lah too-saN
Ascension	l'Ascension *f* lah-sahN-see-ohN
Assumption	l'Assomption *f* lah-sohN-see-ohN
Christmas	Noël no-el
Christmas Day	Noël (le vingt-cinq décembre) no-el (luh vaN-saNk day-sahN-bruh)
Christmas Eve	la veille de Noël lah veh-yuh duh no-el
Corpus Christi	la fête du Saint Sacrement lah fet dew saN sah-kruh-mahN
Easter	Pâques pahk
Easter Monday	le lundi de Pâques luh laN-dee duh pahk
Good Friday	le vendredi-saint luh vahN-druh-dee saN
Labor Day (May 1)	la Fête du Travail lah fet dew trah-vah
Mardi Gras	le mardi gras luh mahr-dee grah
New Year's Day	le jour de l'an luh zhoor duh-lahN
New Year's Eve	la Saint-Sylvestre lah saN-seel-ves-truh
Pentecost	la Pentecôte lah pahNt-kawt

Weather
and
Environment

What's the weather going to be like today?
Quel temps va-t-il faire aujourd'hui?

Can you drink the water?
Est-ce que l'eau est potable?

Weather

What *nice / terrible* weather we're having today!	Quel *beau / mauvais* temps, aujourd'hui! kel *bo / mo-veh* tahN o-zhoor-dwee
What's the weather going to be like *today / tomorrow*?	Quel temps va-t-il faire *aujourd'hui / demain*? kel tahN vah-teel fehr *o-zhoor-dwee / duh-maN*
What's the weather forecast?	Que dit la météo? kuh dee lah may-teh-o
It is / It's going to be …	Il *fait / va faire* … eel *feh / vah fehr*
– nice.	– beau. bo
– bad.	– mauvais. mo-veh
– warm.	– chaud. sho
– hot.	– très chaud. treh sho
– cold.	– froid. frwah
– humid.	– lourd. loor
It's going to *rain / be stormy*.	Il va y avoir *de la pluie / un orage*. eel vah ee ah-vwahr *duh lah plwee / aN aw-rahzh*
The sun's shining.	Le soleil brille. luh so-lay bree-yuh
It's pretty windy.	Il y a pas mal de vent. eel yah pah mahl duh vahN
It's raining.	Il pleut. eel pluh
It's snowing.	Il neige. eel nehzh
What's the temperature?	Quelle est la température? kel eh lah tahN-pehr-ah-tewr
It's … degrees (below zero).	Il fait … degrés (au-dessous de zéro). eel feh … duh-gray (o duh-soo duh zeh-ro)

Weather: Additional Words

clear	clair klehr
climate	le climat luh klee-mah
cloud	le nuage luh new-ahzh
cloudy	nuageux new-ah-zhuh
cool	frais f, fraîche pl freh fresh
damp	humide ew-meed
dawn	l'aube f lobe
degrees	le degré luh duh-gray
drizzle	le crachin luh krah-shaN
dry	sec f, sèche pl sek sesh
dusk	le crépuscule luh kray-pews-kewl
fog	le brouillard luh broo-yahr
frost	le gel luh zhel
hail	la grêle lah grel
hazy	brumeux brew-muh
heat	la grosse chaleur lah gross shah-luhr
lightning	l'éclair m lay-klehr
moon	la lune lah lewn
rainy	pluvieux plew-vyuh
shower	l'averse f lah-vehrss
snow	la neige lah nehzh
star	l'étoile f lay-twahl
sun	le soleil luh so-lay
sunny	ensoleillé ahN-so-leh-yeh
thunder	le tonnerre luh tun-ehr
variable	capricieux kah-pree-see-uh
wet	mouillé moo-yeh
wind	le vent luh vahN

Environment

It's very loud here.

Ici, c'est très bruyant.
ee-see seh treh brew-yahN

Could you please shut off that noise?

Est-ce que vous pouvez arrêter ce bruit? es kuh voo poo-veh ah-ret-teh suh brew-ee

It smells bad here.

Ça ne sent pas très bon, ici.
sah nuh sahN pah treh bohN ee-see

Where's that smell coming from?

D'où vient cette odeur?
doo-vee-aN set o-duhr

Can you drink the water?

Est-ce que l'eau est potable?
es kuh lo eh po-tah-bluh

The *water* / *air* is polluted.

L'eau / *L'air* est pollué(e).
lo / *lehr* eh pawl-eweh

Is that dangerous?

Est-ce que c'est dangereux?
es kuh seh dahN-zheh-ruh

Grammar

Verbs and Their Tenses

There are three verb types that follow a regular pattern, their infinitives ending in -er, -ir and -re, e.g. to speak, par<u>ler</u>, to finish, fin<u>ir</u>, to return, ren<u>dre</u>. Here are the most commonly used present, past and future forms.

	Present	Past	Future
je / j' *I*	parle	ai parlé	parlerai
tu *you* (informal)	parles	as parlé	parleras
il / elle *he / she*	parle	a parlé	parlera
nous *we*	parlons	avons parlé	parlerons
vous *you*	parlez	avez parlé	parlerez
ils / elles *they*	parlent	ont parlé	parleront
je / j' *I*	finis	ai fini	finirai
tu *you* (informal)	finis	as fini	finiras
il / elle *he / she*	finit	a fini	finira
nous *we*	finissons	avons fini	finirons
vous *you*	finissez	avez fini	finirez
ils / elles *they*	finissent	ont fini	finiront
je / j' *I*	rends	ai rendu	rendrai
tu *you* (informal)	rends	as rendu	rendras
il / elle *he / she*	rend	a rendu	rendra
nous *we*	rendons	avons rendu	rendrons
vous *you*	rendez	avez rendu	rendrez
ils / elles *they*	rendent	ont rendu	rendront

Examples: J'aime la musique.   I like music.
Parlez-vous anglais? Do you speak English?

There are many irregular verbs whose forms differ considerably. The most common way to express the past is by using the conjugated form of *to have*, avoir, and the past participle of the verb as demonstrated below. Many verbs, especially verbs related to movement are conjugated with *to be*, être. In that case the participle agrees with number and gender of the subject.

avoir to have	être to be
j'ai I have	je suis I am
tu as you have	tu es you are
il / elle a he / she has	il / elle est he / she is
nous avons we have	nous sommes we are
vous avez you have	vous êtes you are
ils / elles ont they have	ils / elles sont they are

Examples: Nous avons visité Paris.
We visited Paris.
Elle est arrivée en retard.
She arrived late.
Elles sont allées au cinéma.
They (fem.) went to the movies.

Imperatives (Command Form)

Imperative sentences are formed by using the stem of the verb with the appropriate ending.

tu you (informal)	Parle! Speak!
nous we	Parlons! Let's speak!
vous you	Parlez! Speak!
tu you (informal)	Finis! Finish!
nous we	Finissons! Let's finish!
vous you	Finissez! Finish!

Nouns and Their Determiners

In French, nouns are either masculine (m) or feminine (f).
Generally, nouns ending in -e, -té and -tion are feminine. The
definite articles are le (m) and la (f). In the plural (pl.) (les) the
endings are -s or -x but the final s or x is not pronounced.

Examples: Singular <u>le</u> train the train   <u>la</u> table the table
          Plural   <u>les</u> trains the trains   <u>les</u> tables the tables

The indefinite articles also indicate gender: un (m), une (f),
des (pl. m and f).

Examples: Singular <u>un</u> livre a book   Plural <u>des</u> livres books

          <u>une</u> porte a door   <u>des</u> portes doors

Possessive adjectives agree in gender and number with their noun:

	Masculine	Feminine	Plural
my	mon	ma	mes
your	ton	ta	tes
his / her / its	son	sa	ses
our	notre	notre	nos
your	votre	votre	vos
their	leur	leur	leurs

Examples: Je cherche <u>leurs</u> clés.   I'm looking for their keys.
            Où est <u>votre</u> billet?   Where is your ticket?
            C'est <u>ma</u> place.   That's my seat.

Adjectives

Adjectives describe nouns. They agree with the noun in gender and number. Most of them form the feminine by adding -e to the masculine unless the word already ends in -e. For the plural, add -s. Most adjectives follow the noun.

Examples: J'ai une auto américaine. I have an American car
Mon patron est agréable. My boss is nice.

Comparatives and Superlatives

Comparatives and superlatives are formed by adding more, plus, less, moins, the most le / la plus or the least le / la moins before the adjective.

Adjective	Comparative	Superlative
grand	plus grand(e)	le / la / les plus grand(e)(s)
big	bigger	the biggest
cher	moins cher	le / la / les moins cher(s) / chère(s)
cheap	cheaper	cheapest

Example: Où est la pharmacie la plus proche?
Where is the nearest pharmacy?

Adverbs and Adverbial Expressions

Adverbs describe verbs. They are often formed by adding -ment to the feminine form of the adjective.

Examples: Jean conduit lentement. Jean drives slowly.
Robert conduit rapidement. Robert drives fast.

Some common adverbial time expressions:

tout de suite	immediately
pas encore	not yet
encore	still
avant	before
déjà	already
ne ... jamais	never

Pronouns

Possessive Pronouns

Pronouns serve as substitutes for nouns and relate to number and gender.

	Singular	Plural
mine	le mien / la mienne	les miens / les miennes
yours (inf.)	le tien / la tienne	les tiens / les tiennes
his / her / its	*le sien / la sienne*	*les siens / les siennes*
ours	le / la nôtre	les nôtres
yours	le / la vôtre	les vôtres
theirs	le / la leur	les leurs

Examples: Nos passeports? <u>Le mien</u> est dans mon sac et <u>le tien</u> est dans la valise.

Our passports? Mine is in my bag and yours is in the suitcase.

----- Grammar -----

Demonstrative Pronouns

The following are used to differentiate <u>this</u> and <u>that</u>:

this one	celui-ci (sing. m)	celle-ci (sing. f)
that one	celui-là (sing. m)	celle-là (sing. f)
these	ceux-ci (pl. m)	celles-ci (pl. f)
those	ceux-là (pl. m)	celles-là (pl. f)

Examples: <u>Celui-ci</u> coûte moins cher. This one costs less.
Je préfère <u>celle-là</u>.   I prefer that one.

Word Order

The conjugated verb comes after the subject.

Example: Nous habitons à Lyon.   We live in Lyon.

Questions are formed by simply raising your voice at the end of the sentence, by adding Est-ce que before the sentence or by reversing the order of subject and verb. Subject and verb must be reversed when using key question words like *where*, où.

Examples: Vous avez des cartes?   Do you have maps?
Est-ce que tu es en vacances?   Are you on vacation?
Où est la banque?   Where is the bank?

Negations

Negative sentences are generally formed by adding ne before the verb and pas after it.

Examples: Nous ne fumons <u>pas</u>.   We don't smoke.
Ce <u>n'</u>est pas neuf.   It's not new.
Tu <u>n'</u>as <u>pas</u> acheté ça?   You didn't buy that?

209

Conversion Charts

The following conversion charts contain the most commonly used measures.

1 Gramme (g)	= 1000 milligrams	= 0.035 oz.
1 Livre (lb)	= 500 grams	= 1.1 lb
1 Kilogramme (kg)	= 1000 grams	= 2.2 lb
1 Litre (l)	= 1000 milliliters	= 1.06 U.S / 0.88 Brit. quarts
		= 2.11 /1.8 US /Brit. pints
		= 34 /35 US /Brit. fluid oz.
1 Centimètre (cm)	= 10 millimeter	= 0.4 inch
1 Mètre (m)	= 100 centimeters	= 39.37 inches/3.28 ft.
1 Kilomètre (km)	= 1000 meters	= 0.62 mile
1 Mètre carrè (qm)	= 10.8 square feet	
1 Hectare (ha)	= 10000 sq meters	= 2.5 acres
1 Kilomètre carrè (km^2)	= 247 acres	

Not sure whether to put on a bathing suit or a winter coat? Here is a comparison of Fahrenheit and and Celsius / Centigrade degrees.

-40°C – -40°F	-1° C – 30° F	20° C – 68° F	
-30°C – -22°F	0° C – 32° F	25° C – 77° F	
-20°C – -4° F	5° C – 41° F	30° C – 86° F	
-10°C – 14° F	10° C – 50° F	35° C – 95° F	
-5° C – 23° F	15° C – 59° F		

When you know	Multiply by	To find
ounces	28.3	grams
pounds	0.45	kilograms
inches	2.54	centimeters
feet	0.3	meters
miles	1.61	kilometers
square inches	6.45	sq. centimeters
square feet	0.09	sq. meters
square miles	2.59	sq. kilometers
pints (US/Brit)	0.47 / 0.56	liters
gallons (US/Brit)	3.8 / 4.5	liters

**Travel Dictionary
English – French**

A

a little un peu aN puh

a month ago il y a un mois eel yah aN mwah

abbey abbaye *f* ah-bay

abdomen ventre *m* uh vahN-truh

abscess abcès *m* ahb-seh

accident accident *m* ahk-see-dahN

accident report constat à l'a-miable *m* luh kohN-stah ah lah-mee-ah-bluh

act acte *m* ahkt

actor acteur *m* ahk-tuhr

actress actrice *f* ahk-treess

acupuncture acupuncture *f* ah-kew-pohNk-tewr

adapter adaptateur *m* ah-dahp-tuhr

address adresse *f* ah-dress

addressee destinataire *m* des-tee-nah-tehr

adhesive bandage pansement *m* pahNs-mahN

adults adultes ah-dewlt

advance booking réservation *f* ray-sehr-vah-see-ohN

aerial tramway téléphérique *m* teh-lay-feh-reek

after derrière dehr-ee-ehr

after sunburn lotion pomma-de contre les coups de soleil *f* pum-ahd kohN-truh lay koo duh so-lay

afternoon après-midi *m* ah-preh-mee-dee

age époque *f* ay-pawk

AIDS sida *m* see-dah

air air *m* lehr

air conditioning climatisation *f* klee-mah-tee-sah-see-ohN

air filter filtre à air *m* feel-truh ah ehr

air mattress matelas pneuma-tique *m* maht-lah pnuh-mah-teek

airport aéroport *m* ah-ehr-o-por

airport shuttle bus navette (d'aéroport) *f* ah nah-vet dah-ehr-o-por

airport tax taxe d'aéroport *f* ah tahx dah-ehr-o-por

alarm clock réveil *m* ray-veh

alcohol-free sans alcool sahN-zahl-cawl

allergy allergie *f* ah-lehr-zhee

allergy-tested anallergique ahn-ahl-ehr-zheek

alone seul suhl

altar autel *m* o-tel

alternator dynamo *f* dee-nah-mo

aluminum foil aluminium *m* ménager lew-meen-yum may-nah-zheh

amalgam filling amalgame *m* lah-mahl-gahm

amount montant *m* mohN tahN

ankle cheville *f* sheh-vee

anorak anorak *m* ah-naw-rahk

anti-itch cream pommade contre les démangeaisons *f* pum-ahd kohN-truh lay day-mahN-zheh-zohN

antibiotic antibiotique *m* ahN-tee-bee-o-teek

antifreeze antigel *m* ahN-tee-zhel

antique antiquité *f* ahN-teek-kee-teh

antique shop magasin d'an-tiquités *m* mah-gah-zaN dahN-tee-kee-teh

antiseptic désinfectant *m* day-saN-fek-tahN

apartment studio *m* stew-dyoh

appendicitis appendicite *f* ah-pahN-dee-seet

appendix appendice *m* ah-pahN-deess

appetizer entrée *f* ahN-treh

apple pomme *f* pum

apple cider (alcoholic) cidre *m* see-druh

apple juice jus de pomme *m* zhew duh pum

applications indications thérapeutiques aN-dee-kah-see-ohN tehr-ah-puh-teek

apricot abricot *m* ahb-ree-ko

April avril ah-vreel

aqueduct aqueduc *m* ah-kuh-dewk

architect architecte *m* ahr-shee-tekt

area région *f* ray-zhee-ohN

arm bras *m* brah

arm floats brassards *m/pl* de natation brah-sahr duh nah-tah-see-ohN

armchair fauteuil *m* fo-tuh-yuh

to arrest arrêter ah-reh-teh

arrival arrivée *f* ah-ree-veh

to arrive arriver ah-ree-veh

art art *m* ahr

art collection collection de peintures *f* ko-ek-see-ohN duh paN-tewr

artichoke artichaut *m* ahr-tee-sho

artist artiste *m, f* ahr-teest

arts and crafts artisanat *m* ahr-tee-sahn-ah

ashtray cendrier *m* sahN-dree-yeh

asparagus asperge *f* ah-spehrzh

asthma asthme *m* ahsm

August août oot

automatic teller machine (ATM) distributeur de billets *m* dee-stree-bew-tuhr duh bee-yeh

avalanche avalanche *f* ah-vah-lahNsh

avocado avocat *m* ah-vo-kah

axle essieu *m* ess-yuh

B

baby bottle biberon *m* bee-buh-rohN

baby food aliments *m/pl* pour bébés ah-lee-mahN poor bay-bay

baby powder poudre pour bébés *f* poo-druh poor bay-bay

back retour ruh-toor

back light feu arrière *m* fuh ah-ree-yehr

backpack sac à dos *m* sahk ah doh

badminton badminton *m* bahd-mee-tohN

badminton racket raquette de badminton *f* rah-ket duh bahd-meen-tohN

bag sac *m* sahk

baggage claim retrait des bagages *m* ruh-treh day bah-gahzh

baggage storage consigne *f* kohN-seen-yuh

baked cuit au four kwee oh foor

bakery boulangerie *f* boo-lahN-zheh-ree

balcony galerie *f* gal-uh-ree

ball ballon *m* aN bah-lohN

ballet ballet *m* bah-leh

ballooning ballon *m* bah-lohN

balsamic vinegar vinaigre balsamique *m* vee-nehg-ruh bahl-sah-meek

212

banana banane f bah-nahn
band groupe m group
bangs frange f frahNzh
bar bar m bahr
barometric pressure pression atmosphérique f pres-see-ohN aht-mos-feh-reek
baroque baroque m bah-rawk
barrette barrette f bah-ret
basil basilic m bah-see-leek
basketball basket m bahs-ket
bathing suit maillot de bain m mah-yoh duh baN
bathrobe peignoir m (de bain) pen-ywahr
bathtub baignoire f ben-wahr
battery batterie f bah-tuh-ree
battery pile f peel
beach plage f plahzh
beach ball ballon de plage m bah-lohN duh plahzh
beach hat chapeau de soleil m shah-po-duh so-lay
beach volleyball beach-volley m beach-vawl-eh
beard barbe f bahrb
bed lit m lee
bed linen draps m/pl drah
bedspread couverture f koo-vehr-tewr
beef bœuf m buhf
beer bière f bee-yehr
before devant duh-vahN
behind derrière dehr-ee-ehr
beige beige behzh
bell cloche f klawsh
bell pepper poivron m pwah-vrohN
bell tower clocher m klaw-shay
belt ceinture f saN-tewr
bend virage m vee-rahzh
beret béret (basque) m bay-ray bahsk
beside à côté de ah ko-teh duh

bicycle repair kit set de réparation pour vélo m set duh ray-pah-rah-see-ohN poor veh-lo
bigger plus grand plew grahN
bike basket panier porte-bagages m pahn-yeh pawt-bah-gahzh
bikini bikini m bee-kee-nee
bill facture f fahk-tewr
binding fixation f feex-ah-see-ohN
birth control pill pilule contraceptive f pee-lewl kohN-trah-sep-teev
bite morsure f mawr-sewr
bite piqûre f pee-kewr
black noir nwahr
black ice verglas m vehr-glah
blackcurrant liqueur cassis m kah-seess
bladder vessie f ves-see
blanket couverture f koo-vehr-tewr
blazer blazer m blay-zehr
blind nonvoyant m/ nonvoyante f/ aveugle nohN-vwah-yahN / nohN-vwah-yahNt ah-vuh-gluh
blister vessie f ves-see
blond m, **blonde** f blond blohN
blood sang m sahN
blood poisoning f septicémie sep-tee-say-mee
blood sausage boudin m noir boo-daN nwahr
blouse chemisier m shuh-mee-zee-yeh
to blow-dry faire un brushing fehr aN bruh-shing
blue bleu bluh
blue cheese bleu m bluh
blush blush m blush
boarding pass carte d'embarquement f kahrt dahN-bahrk-mahN

boat rentals location de bateaux f lo-kah-see-ohN duh bah-to
body corps m kawr
body lotion lotion corporelle f lo-see-ohN kor-por-el
boiled cuit à l'eau kwee a lo
bone os m oss
bookstore librairie f lee-breh-ree
boots bottes f/pl bawt
border frontière f frohN-tyehr
botanical garden jardin botanique m zhar-daN bo-tah-neek
bottle bouteille f boo-teh-yuh
bottle opener décapsuleur m day-kahp-sewl-uhr
bottle warmer chauffe-biberon m shohf-bee-buh-rohN
bottom séant m say-ahN
boutique boutique f boo-teek
bowl (salad) saladier m sah-lahd-yeh
bowl bol m bawl
bowling alley bowling m bowling
box loge f lawzh
box office caisse f kess
boy garçon m gah-sohN
boyfriend ami m ah-mee
bra soutien-gorge m soo-tee-aN gawrzh
bracelet bracelet m brahss-lay
braces appareil m dentaire ah-pah-ray dahN-tehr
brain cerveau m sehr-vo
brake frein m fraN
brake fluid liquide des freins m lee-keed day fraN
brake light feu de stop m fuh duh stawp
bread pain m paN
breaded pané pah-nay

breakfast petit déjeuner m puh-tee day-zhuh-nay
breakfast buffet buffet du petit déjeuner m bew-feh dew puh-tee day-zhuh-nay
breakfast room salle du petit déjeuner f sahl dew puh-tee day-zhuh-nay
brewery brasserie f brahs-suh-ree
bridge pont m pohN
briefs pl slip m sleep
bright beau bo
broccoli brocoli m braw-kaw-lee
brochure catalogue m kah-tah-lawg
broken cassé kah-say
bronchial tubes bronches f/pl brohNsh
bronchitis bronchite f brawn-sheet
brooch broche f brawsh
broom balai m bah-lay
brother frère m frehr
brothers and sisters frères et sœurs m/pl frehr eh suhr
brown marron mah-rohN
brown brun braN
bruise contusion f kohN-tew-zee-ohN
brush brosse f brawss
Brussels sprouts choux m/pl de Bruxelles shoo duh brewx-el
bucket seau m soh
building édifice m ay-dee-feess
bulb ampoule f ahN-pool
bumper pare-chocs m pahr-shohk
bungalow bungalow m bahN-gah-lo
bungee jumping saut à l'élastique m so-tah lay-lahs-teek
bunk beds lits m/pl superposés lee sew-pehr-po-say

burgundy rouge foncé roozh fohN-say
burn brûlure *f* brew-lewr
bus station gare routière *f* gah roo-tyehr
bus stop arrêt *m* de bus ah-ray duh bewss
bust buste *m* bewst
butcher's boucherie *f* boosh-u h-ree
butter beurre *m* buhr
to buy acheter ahsh-teh
bypass by-pass *m* by-pass

C

cabaret cabaret *m* kah-bah-reh
cabbage chou *m* shoo
cable câble *m* kah-bluh
cake gâteau *m* gah-to
cake, tart gâteau *m* gah-toh
calf mollet *m* maw-leh
camcorder caméscope *m* kahm-eh-skawkp
camelhair poil de chameau *m* pwahl duh shah-mo
to camp camper kahN-per
camping camping *m* kahN-ping
campsite terrain de camping *m* tehr-aN duh kahN-ping
can opener ouvre-boîte *m* oo-vruh bwaht
cancer cancer *m* kahN-sehr
candles bougies *f/pl* boo-zhee
candy store confiserie *f* kohN-fee-seh-ree
canned foods conserves *f/pl* kohN-sehrv
canned sardines sardines *f/pl* à l'huile sahr-deen ah lweel
canoe canoë *m* kah-noh-eh
capital capitale *f* kah-pee-tahl
captain capitaine *m* kah-pee-ten
car voiture *f* vwah-tewr

car ferry car-ferry *m* kahr-feh-ree
car key clé de la voiture *f* klay duh lah vwah-tewr
car radio autoradio *m* o-toh-rah-dyo
car seat siège pour enfant *m* see-ehzh poor ahN-fahN
carat carat *m* kah-rah
carbonated mineral water eau *f* minérale gazeuse oh meen-eh-rahl gah-zuhz
carburetor carburateur *m* kah-bew-rah-tuhr
card number numéro de la carte *m* new-may-ro duh lah kahrt
cardiac infarction infarctus *m* aN-fahrk-tewss
carp carpe *f* kahrp
carrots carottes *f/pl* kah-rawt
carry-on bagages *m/pl* à main bah-gahzh ah maN
carving sculpture sur bois *f* skewlp-tewr sewr bwah
cash transfer virement (bancaire) *m* veer-mahN bahN-kehr
cashmere cachemire *m* kahsh-meer
casino casino *m* kah-zee-no
cassette cassette *f* kah-set
castle château fort *m* shah-to fawr
castle château *m* shah-toh
catalytic converter pot catalytique *m* poh kah-tah-leek-teek
cathedral cathédrale *f* kah-teh-drahl
Catholic catholique kah-toh-leek
cauliflower chou *m* fleur shoo fluhr
cave grotte *f* grawt
cavity carie *f* kah-ree

215

CD/DVD CD/DVD *m* say-day / day-veh-day

ceiling plafond *m* plah-fohN

cell phone portable *m*

Celtic celtique sel-teek

cemetery cimetière *m* seem-tyehr

center milieu *m* mee-lyuh

century siècle *m* see-ek-luh

ceramic céramique *f* seh-rah-meek

cereal muesli *m* mews-lee

certificate certificat *m* sehr tee-fee-kah

chair chaise *f* shez

chair lift télésiège *m* teh-lay-see-yehzh

champagne champagne *m* shaN-pahn-yuh

changing room cabine *f* kah-been

chapel chapelle *f* shah-pel

charcoal charbon de bois *m* shahr-bohN duh bwah

charcoal tablets comprimés *m/pl* de charbon kohN-pree-may duh shahr-bohN

cheap cher mwahN-shehr

check chèque *m* shek

to check in enregistrer ahN-reh-zhees-treh

check-in déclaration de séjour *f* day-klah-rah-see-ohN duh say-zhoor

check-in desk guichet *m* gee-sheh

cheese fromage *m* fro-mahzh

cheese platter plateau *m* de fromages plah-toh duh fro-mahzh

chemical toilet toilettes chimiques *f/pl* twah-let shee-meek

cherries cerises *f/pl* sehr-eez

chest poitrine *f* pwah-treen

chicken poulet *m* poo-lay

chicken breast blanc *m* de poulet blahN duh poo-leh

chicken pox varicelle *f* vah-ree sel

chicory endive *f* ahN-deev

child enfant *m* ahN-fahN

child safety belt ceinture de sécurité pour enfants *f* sahN-tewr duh say-kewr-ee teh poor ahN-fahN

child seat siège pour enfant *m* see-yehzh poor ahN-fahN

children's portion assiette *f* pour enfants ahs-syet poor ahN-fahN

child's bicycle vélo pour enfant *m* veh-lo poor ahN-fahN

chili pepper piment *m* pee mahN

chills frissons *m/pl* frees-sohN

chimes carillon *m* kah-ree-yohN

chives *m/pl* ciboulettes see-boo-let

chocolate chocolat *m* sho-ko-lah

chocolate ice cream glace *f* au chocolat glahss oh sho-ko-lah

choir chœur *m* kuhr

(pork, lamb) chop côtelette de porc/d'agneau *f* kawt-uh-let duh pawr/dah-nyo

church église *f* ay-gleez

church service office *m* religieux law-feess ruh-lee-zhyuh

church tower clocher *m* klaw-shay

cigarillos cigarillos *m/pl* see-gah-ree-yos

cigars cigares *m/pl* see-gahr

circulatory problems troubles *m/pl* circulatoires troo-bluh seer-kew-lah-twahr

circus cirque *m* seerk

city center centre-ville *m* sahN-truh veel

class classe *f* klahss

classical; ancient antique ahN-teek

cleaning products produits *m/pl* de nettoyage pro-dwee duh net-wah-yazh

cleansing nettoyage *m* net-wah-yahzh

clear clair klehr

clear broth consommé *m* kohN-so-may

climate climat *m* klee-mah

to climb escalader es-kah-lah-day

climbing boots chaussures *f/pl* de montagne sho-sewr duh mohN-tahn-yuh

clip-on earrings boucles *f/pl* d'oreille à clips boo-kluh do-ray ah kleep

cloisters *pl* cloître *m* klwah-truh

closed fermé fehr-may

cloth chiffon *m* shee-fohN

clothes pins pinces *f/pl* à linge paNs ah laNzh

cloud nuage *m* new-ahzh

cloudy nuageux new-ah-zhuh

clutch embrayage *m* ahN-bray-ahzh

coast côte f kote

coat manteau *m* mahN-toh

coat of arms armes f zahrm

coatroom vestiaire *m* ves-tehr

cocktail cocktail *m* kawk-tail

cocoa cacao *m* kah-kah-oh

cod cabillaud *m* kah-bee-yoh

coffee café *m* kah-feh

coffee-maker cafetière f (électrique) kah-feh-tyehr

coin pièce f pee-ess

cold froid frwah

cold rhume *m* rewm

cold cuts *pl* charcuterie f shahr-kew-tree

colic colique f kaw-leek

collarbone clavicule f klah-vee-kewl

collection collection f ko-lek-see-ohN

colorful multicolore mewl-tee-ko-lawr

coloring book livre de coloriage *m* leev-ruh duh koh-lohr-ee-ahzh

comb peigne *m* pen-yuh

to come back revenir ruh-vuh-neer

companion accompagnateur *m*/ l'accompagnatrice f ah-kohN-pahn-yah-tuhr/ lah-kohN-pahn-yah-treess

compartment compartiment *m* kohN-pahr-tee-mahN

complaint réclamation f ray-klah-mah-see-ohN

complete meal menu *m* muh-new

compose composer kohN-po-zeh

composer compositeur *m*/ compositrice f kohN-poz-ee-tuhr/ kohN-poz-ee-treess

composite filling composite *m* kohN-po-zeet

concussion commotion cérébrale f kohM-mo-see-ohN say-ray-brahl

condoms préservatifs *m/pl* pray-sehr-vah-teef

conductor (train) contrôleur *m* luh kohN-tro-luhr

conductor chef d'orchestre *m* shef daw-kes-truh

conjunctivitis conjonctivite f kohN-zhohNd-tee-veet

connecting flight correspondance f kaw-rehs-pohN-dahNs

connection correspondance f kaw-res-pohN-dahNs

constipation constipation *f* kohN-stee-pah-see-ohN

contraindications contre-indications kohN-truh-aN-dee kah see-ohN

convent couvent *m* koo-vahN

cookbook livre de cuisine *m* lee-vruh duh kwee-zeen

cooked ham jambon *m* blanc zhahN-bohN blahN

cookies biscuits *m/pl* beess-kwee

cool frais, *f:* fraîche freh fresh

coolant liquide de refroidissement *m* lee-keed duh ruh-fwah-deess-mahN

cooler glacière *f* glah-syehr

copy copie *f* kaw-pee

corkscrew tire-bouchon *m* teer-boo-shohN

corn maïs *m* mah-eess

to cost coûter koo-teh

costume jewelry bijou fantaisie *m* bee-zhoo fahN-teh-zee

cot (for a child) lit d'enfant *m* lee dahN-fahN

cotton coton *m* koh-tohN

cotton balls coton *m* ko-tohN

cotton swabs Cotons-Tiges *m/pl* ® ko-tohN-teeg

cough toux *f* too

cough medicine sirop contre la toux *m* see-ro kohN-truh lah too

counter caisse *f* kess

counter (window) guichet *m* gee-shay

counterfeit money fausse monnaie *f* fohss mun-ay

country pays *m* pay-ee

country road route départementale *f* root day-paht-mahN-tahl

course plat *m* plah

court cour *f* koor

cover couvert *m* koo-vehr

crab crabe *m* krahb

cramp crampe *f* krahNp

crampon crampons *m/pl* krahN-pohN

crash tamponnement *m* tahN-pun-mahN

crayon crayon de pastel *m* kray-ohN de pah-stel

cream crème *f* krem

cream puff chou *m* à la crème shoo ah lah krem

credit card carte de crédit *f* kahrt duh kray-dee

crockery, tableware vaisselle *f* veh-sel

croissant croissant *m* krwah-sahN

cross croix *f* krwah

cross-country skiing ski de fond *m* ski duh fohN

cruise croisière *f* krwah-zee-ehr

crutch béquille *f* bay-kee-yuh

crème caramel crème *f* caramel krem kah-rah-mel

cucumber concombre *m* kohN-kohN-bruh

cucumber salad salade *f* de concombres sah-lahd duh kohN-kohN-bruh

cup, goblet gobelet *m* gawb-lay

cup, mug tasse *f* tahss

curling curling *m* kuhr-ling

curls boucles *f/pl* (de cheveux) boo-kluh duh shuh-vuh

currency valeur *f* vah-luhr

currency exchange bureau de change *m* bew-ro duh chahNzh

curve virage *m* vee-rahzh

customs douane *f* dwahn

customs declaration déclaration de douane *f* day-klah-ra-see ohN duh dwahn

cycling path piste cyclable *f* peest see-kleest

cystitis cystite *f* sees-teet

D

damp humide ew-meed
dance soirée dansante f swah-ray dahN-sahNt
dancer danseur m / danseuse f dahN-suhr/dahN-suhz
dandruff pellicules f/pl pel-ee-kewl
dark beer bière f brune bee-yehr brewn
dates dattes f/pl daht
daughter fille f fee
dawn aube f obe
day jour m zhoor
deaf sourd m/sourde f soor/so-ord
December décembre day-sahN-bruh
deck pont m pohN
deckchair chaise longue f shehz lohNg
declaration of value valeur déclarée f vah-uhr day-klah-ray
degrees degré m duh-gray
delay retard m ruh-tahr
delete supprimer sew-pree-may
delicatessen l'épicerie f fine lay-pee-suh-ree feen
delighted enchanté ahN-shahN-teh
dental floss fil dentaire m feel dahN-tehr
dentist dentiste m dahN-teest
dentures pl dentier m dahN-tee-eh
deodorant déodorant m day oh-daw-rahN
department store grand magasin m grahN mah-gah-zaN
departure départ m day-pahr
deposit acompte m ahcohNt
deposit caution f ko-see-ohN

dermatologist dermatologue m dehr-mah-toh-lawg
dessert dessert m day-sehr
detective novel policier m paw-lee-see-eh
detergent détergent m day-tehr-zhahN
detergent lessive f les-seev
diabetes diabète m dee-ah-bet
diamond diamant m dee-ah-mahN
diarrhea diarrhée f dee-ah-ray
dictionary dictionnaire m deek-see-ohN-nehr
diet régime m ray-zheem
digestif (brandy) digestif m dee-zhes-teef
digital camera l'appareil m photo numérique lah-pah-ray fo-toh new-mehr-eek
dining car wagon-restaurant m vah-gohN-res-toh-rahN
dining room salle à manger f sahl ah mahN-zheh
dinner dîner m dee-nay
direction direction f dee-rek-see-ohN
directions recette ruh-set:
dirty sale sahl
disc disque intervertébral m deesk aN-tehr-vehr-teh-brahl
disease maladie f mah-lah dee
dishes vaisselle f veh-sel
dishtowel lavette f lah-vet
dishwashing detergent liquide vaisselle m lee-keed veh-sel
dislocated luxé lewx-eh
to dive plonger plohN-zheh
diving equipment l'équipement m de plongée lay-keep-mahN duh plohN-zheh
diving mask lunettes f/pl de plongée lewn-et duh plohN-zheh

diving suit combinaison de plongée *f* kohN-bee-nay-zohN duh plohN-zheh

dizziness vertiges *m/pl* vehr-teezh

dock point d'accostage *m* pwahN dah-kaws-tahzh

doctor médecin *m* made-saN

documents papiers *m/pl* pah-pyeh

dome coupole *f* koo-pohl

dormitory dortoir *m* daw-twah

dosage instructions posologie *f* pos-o-lo-zhee

double double *m* doo-bluh

double bed lit conjugal *m* lee kohN-zhew-gahl

down the steps en bas de l'escalier ahN bah duh less-kahl-yeh

Draft brouillons *m/pl* broo-yohN

draft beer bière *f* pression bee-yehr pres-see-ohN

drag lift téléski *m* teh-lay-ski

drain l'écoulement lay-kool-mahN

drawing dessin *m* day-saN

dress robe *f* rawb

dressing vinaigrette *f* vee-neh-gret

to drink boire bwahr

drink boisson *f* bwah-sohN

drinking water l'eau *f* potable lo po-tah-bluh

to drive conduire kohN-dweer

driver chauffeur *m* shoh-fuhr

driver's license permis de conduire *m* pehr-mee-duh kohN-dweer

drizzle crachin *m* krah-shaN

drops gouttes *f/pl* goot

dry sec, *f*: sèche sek sesh

dry (champagne) brut brew

dry cleaner's pressing *m* pres-sing

dryer sèche-linge *m* sehsh-laNzh

dubbed postsynchronisé pa-wst-saN-kro-nee-zeh

duffle bag sac de marin *m* sahk duh mah-raN

dumpling quenelle *f* kuh-nel

dusk crépuscule *m* kray-pews-cewl

dust poussière *f* poos-yehr

to dye faire une teinture fehr ewn taN-tewr

E

ear oreille *f* o-ray

ear drops gouttes *f/pl* pour les oreilles goot poor lay-zo-ray

ear, nose and throat doctor oto-rhino-laryngologiste *m* o-toh-ree-no-lah-raN-go-lo-zheest

early tôt toe

earrings boucles *f/pl* d'oreille boo-kluh do-ray

earthquake tremblement de terre *m* trahN-bluh-mahN duh tehr

to eat manger mahN-zheh

eel anguille *f* ahN-gwee-yuh

egg œuf *m*, *pl*: les œufs uhf lay-zuh

eggplant aubergine *f* o-behr-zheen

elastic bandage bande élastique *f* bahNd eh-lahs-teek

electronics store magasin d'électroménager *m* mah-gah-zaN day-lek-tro-may-nah-zheh

elevator ascenseur *m* ah-sahN-suhr

e-mail courrier électronique *m*

emergency brake frein à main *m* fren ah maN

emergency exit sortie de
  secours *f* sor-tee duh suh-koor
emergency triangle triangle
  de signalisation *m* tree-ahN-
  gluh duh seen-yahl-ee-sah-see-
  ohN
end of season sales soldes *f/pl*
  sawld
endives endives *f/pl*
  ahN-deev
engaged fiancé fee-ahN-say
engine moteur *m* moh-tuhr
engine oil huile *f* moteur
  weel moh-tuhr
envelope enveloppe *f*
  ahN-vel-awp
environmental pollution
  pollution *f* paw-lew-see-ohN
eraser gomme *f* gawm
espresso café *m* express kah-
  feh es-press
essential oil huile *f* parfumée
  weel pah-few-may
evening soir *m* swahr
excavations fouilles *f/pl* foo-
  yuh
exchange rate cours *m* koor
exhaust pot d'échappement *m*
  poh day-shahp-mahN
exhaust fumes gaz
  d'échappement gahz day-
  zhahp-mahN
exhibition exposition *f*
  ek-po-zee-see-ohN
exit sortie *f* saw-tee
expensive cher shehr
express letter lettre exprès *f*
  let-truh ex-press
expressway autoroute
  o-toh-root
extension cord rallonge *f*
  rah-lohNzh
external externe ex-tehrn
eye œil *m, pl:* les yeux
  uh-yuh lay-zyuh
eye drops collyre *m* kawl-leer

eye shadow ombre *f*
  à paupières ohN-bruh ah
  po-pyehr
eye specialist oculiste *m*
  oh-kew-leest
eyeliner crayon khôl *m*
  kray-ohN kohl

F

facade façade *f* fah-sahd
face visage *m* vee-zahzh
face wash lait démaquillant *m*
  lay day-mah-kee-yahN
fall automne *m* o-tun
flashlight lampe de poche *f*
  lahNp duh pawsh
fan ventilateur *m* vahN-tee-lah-
  tuhr
fanbelt courroie *f* koor-wah
fare prix du billet *m* pree dew
  bee-yeh
father père *m* pehr
fatty gras, *f:* grasse
  grah grahss
faucet robinet *m* raw-bee-neh
feature film film *m* feelm
February février feh-vree-eh
felt tip feutre *m* fuh-truh
female doctor médecin *m*
  made-saN
fender aile *f* eh-luh
fennel fenouil *m* fuh-noo-yuh
festival festival *m*
  fes-tee-vahl
feta cheese fromage *m* de
  brebis fro-mahzh duh breh-bee
fever fièvre *f* fee-ev-ruh
fiancé fiancé *m* fee-ahN-say
fiancée fiancée *f* fee-ahN-say
figs figues *f/pl* feeg
fillet of beef filet *m* de bœuf
  fee-lay duh buhf
fillet steak tournedos *m*
  toor-nuh-doh

to film filmer feelm-eh
film camera caméra *f* kah-meh-rah
filter filtre *m* feel-truh
finger doigt *m* dwah
finish laque *f* lahk
fire extinguisher extincteur *m* ex-taNk-tuhr
fireplace cheminée *f* shuh-mee-nay
firewood bois de chauffage *m* bwah duh sho-fahzh
first-aid kit boîte de premiers secours *f* bwaht duh pruhm-yehr suh-koor
fish poisson *m* pwahs-sohN
to fish pêcher peh-sheh
fish bone arête *f* ah-ret
fish soup soupe *f* de poisson soop duh pwah-sohN
fish store poissonnerie *f* pwah-sun-uh-ree
flambé flambé flahN-bay
flash flash *m* flahsh
flea market marché aux puces *m* mahr-shay o pewss
fleece fibre polaire *f* fee-bruh po-lehr
flight vol *m* vol
flight attendant steward *m*/hôtesse *f* de l'air *f* stew-ahr/o-tess duh-lehr
flip-flops sandales *f/pl* de bain sahN-dahl duh baN
flippers palmes *f/pl* pahlm
flood inondation *f* ee-nohN-dah-see-ohN
floor étage *m* ay-tazh
florist fleuriste *m* fluhr-eest
flu grippe *f* greep
flying time durée du vol *f* dew-ray dew vol
foam mattress tapis de sol *m* tah-pee duh sol
fog brouillard *m* broo-yahr

folk museum musée des arts populaires *m* mew-zee day-zahr paw-pewl-lehr
food vivres *m/pl* vee-vruh
food poisoning intoxication *f* alimentaire aN-tawx-ee-kah-see-ohN ah-lee mahN-tehr
foot pied *m* pee-eh
for pour poor
forehead front *m* frohN
forest forêt *f* for-eh
forest fire incendie *m* de forêt aN-sahN-dee duh for-eh
fork fourchette *f* foor-shet
fortress fort *m* fawr
forward faire suivre fehr swee-vruh
fountain fontaine *f* fohN-ten
four-berth cabin cabine à quatre personnes *f* kah-been ah kah-truh pehr-sun
fragrance-free non parfumé nohN pahr-few-may
free libre lee-bruh
free climbing varappe *f* vah-rahp
to freeze; it's freezing geler; il gèle zhel-eh eel zhel
French fries pommes *f/pl* frites pum freet
fresco fresque *f* fresk
fresh frais, *f:* fraîche freh fresh
Friday vendredi vahN-druh-dee
fried eggs œuf *m* au plat uhf oh plah
fried fish friture *f* free-tewr
friend (female) amie *f* ah-mee
friend (male) ami *m* ah-mee
front light feu avant *m* fuh ah-vahN
front mezzanine premier balcon *m* pruhm-yeh bahl-kohN
frost gel *m* zhel

fruit fruits *m/pl* frwee
fruit and vegetable store
épicerie ay-pee-suh-ree
fruit salad macédoine *f* de
fruits mah-seh-dwahn duh
frwee
frying pan poêle *f* pwahl
fungal infection mycose *f*
mee-kawz
funnel entonnoir *m*
ahN-tun-wahr
fuse fusible *m* few-zee-bluh

G

gall bladder bile *f* beel
gallery galerie *f* gah-luh-ree
gallstones calculs *m/pl* biliaires
kah-cewl beel-yehr
game jeu *m* juh
garage garage *m* gah-rahzh
garbage can poubelle *f* poo-
bel
garden jardin *m* zhahr-daN
garlic ail *m* ligh
gas canister cartouche de gaz *f*
kah-toosh duh gahz
gas/petrol station
station-service *f* stah-see-
ohN-sehr-veess
gas stove réchaud à gaz *m*
ray-sho ah gahz
gasket joint *m* zhahN
gate porte *f* pawrt
gauze bandage bande de gaze
f bahNd duh gahz
gear vitesse *f* vee-tess
gel gel *m* zhel
genitals organes *m/pl* génitaux
or-gahn zheh-nee-toh
German measles rubéole *f*
rew-bay-awl
to get off descendre day-sahN-
druh
to get on monter mohN-teh

girl jeune fille *f* zhuhn fee
girlfriend amie *f* ah-mee
glass verre *m* vehr
glider planeur *m* plah-nuhr
gliding vol à voile *m* vawl ah
vwahl
gloves gants *m/pl* gahN
glue colle *f* kawl
goal buts *m/pl* bew
goalkeeper gardien de but *m*
gahr-dee-aN duh bew
goat cheese fromage *m* de
chèvre fro-mahzh duh chehv-
ruh
gold or *m* awr
gold filling plombage en or *m*
plohN-bahzh ahN-awr
gold-plated doré daw-ray
golden doré daw-ray
golf golf *m* gawlf
golf ball balle de golf *f*
bahl duh gawlf
golf club club de golf *m*
cluhb duh gawlf
golf course terrain de golf *m*
tehr-raN duh gawlf
Gothic gothique *m* go-teek
grape raisin *m* ray-saN
grappa, marc marc *m* mahr
grave tombe *f* tohNb
gravy sauce *f* sohss
gray gris gree
green vert vehr
green beans haricots *m/pl*
verts ah-ree-ko vehr
green insurance card carte
verte *f* kahrt vehrt
grill lighter allume-feu *m*
ahl-ewm-fuh
grilled grillé gree-eh
grocery store épicerie *f*
ay-pee-suh-ree
ground meat viande hachée *f*
vee-yahNd ash-eh
guide dog chien d'aveugle *m*
shee-aN dah-vuh-gluh

guinea fowl pintade f
paN-tahd

gum infection inflammation f
de la gencive aN-flah-mah-
see-ohN duh lah zhahN-seev

gums pl gencive f zhahN-seev

gynecologist gynécologue m
gheen-eh-kaw-lawg

haddock églefin m ehg-luh-faN

hail grêle f grel

hair cheveux m/pl shuh-vuh

(elastic) hairband élastique m
à cheveux ay-lahs-teek ah
shuh-vuh

hairclips pinces f/pl à cheveux
pans ah shuh-vuh

hairdresser coiffeur m kwah-
fur

hairspray laque à cheveux f
lahk ah shuh-vuh

hairstyle coiffure f kwah-fewr

hake colin m ko-laN

hall salle f sahl

ham jambon m zhahN-bohN

hammer marteau m mahr-to

hand main f maN

hand brake frein à main m
fraN ah maN

hand cream crème de soins
pour mains f krem duh swan
poor maN

to hand in remettre les
bagages ruh-meh-truh lay
bah-gahzh

hand-carved sculpté à la main
skewlp-teh ah lah maN

handbag sac à main m sahk ah
maN

handball handball m ahNd-
bahl

handmade fait à la main feh
ah lah maN

handpainted peint à la main
paN ah lah maN

hanger cintre m lsaN-truh

harbor port m pawr

hard cider cidre m see-druh

hard-boiled egg œuf m dur
uhf dewr

hardware store quincaillerie f
kaN-kigh-uh-ree

hat chapeau m shah-po

hay fever rhume des foins m
rewm day fwaN

hazy brumeux brew-muh

head tête f tet

headache pills comprimés m/pl
contre le mal de tête kohN-
pree-may kohN-truh luh mahl
duh tet

headlights phare m fah

headphones les écouteurs lay-
zeh-koo-tuhr

hearing impaired
malentendant m/
malentendante f mahl-ahN-
tahN-dahN/mahl-ahN-than-
dahNt

heart cœur m kuhr

heart attack crise cardiaque f
kreez kahr-dee-ahk

heart problem anomalie f
cardiaque ahn-o-mah-lee kahr-
dee-ahk

heartburn brûlures f/pl
(d'estomac) brew-lewr day-
stoh-mah

heat chauffage m show-fahzh

heatwave vague de chaleur f
vahg duh shah-luhr

heel talon m tah-lohN

helmet casque m kahsk

hemorrhage saignement m
sen-yuh-mahN

hemorrhoids hémorroïdes f/pl
em-or-ro-eed

herbal tea infusion f aN-few-
zee-ohN

herbs fines herbes *f/pl* feen-zehrb
here ici ee-see
hernia hernie *f* ehr-nee
herpes herpès *m* ehr-pez
high blood pressure tension, haute *f* tahn-see-ohN oht
high tide marée haute *f* mah-ray oht
high-pressure area anticyclone *m* ahN-tee se-klawn
to hike faire des randonnées fehr day rahN-dun-eh
hiking boots chaussures *f/pl* de montagne sho-sewr duh mohN-tahn-yuh
hiking map carte de randonnées pédestres *f* kahrt duh rahN-dun-eh pay-des-truh
hiking trail sentier de randonnée *m* sahN-tyeh duh rahN-dun-eh
hill colline *f* kaw-leen
hip hanche *f* ahNsh
home fries pommes *f/pl* de terre sautées pum duh tehr so-teh
homemade, traditional-style (fait) maison feh may-zohN
homeopathic homéopathique o-may-o-pah-teek
honey miel *m* mee-yel
hood capot *m* kah-poh
horn klaxon *m* klahx-ohN
hot chaud sho
hot (spicy) épicé eh-pees-say
hot chocolate chocolat *m* chaud sho-ko-lah sho
hotel hôtel *m* o-tel
hour heure *f* uhr
house maison *f* may-sohN
house wine cuvée *f* du patron kew-veh dew pah-trohN
husband mari *m* mah-ree
hut chalet *m* shal-lay

hydrofoil hydroptère *m* ee-drohp-tehr

I

ice cream glace *f* glahss
ID carte d'identité *f* kahrt dee-dahN-tee-teh
ignition allumage *m* ah-lew-mahzh
ignition cable fil d'allumage *m* feel dah-lew-mahzh
impression empreinte *f* ahN-praNt
inbox boîte *f* de réception bwaht duh ray-sep-see-ohN
indigestion tablets comprimés *m/pl* contre les maux d'estomac kohN-ree-may kohN-truh lay moh day-sto-mah
indoor market halles *f/pl* ahl
infection infection *f* aN-fek-see-ohN
infectious contagieux kohN-tah-zhuh
inflammation inflammation *f* aN-flah-mah-see-ohN
information renseignements rahN-sen-yuh-mahN
ingredients composition kohN-po-zee-see-ohN
injection piqûre *f* pee-kewr
injury blessure *f* bles-sewr
inlay inlay *m* een-lay
inner tube chambre à air *f* shahN-bruh ah ehr
inscription inscription *f* aN-screep-see-ohN
insect bite piqûre d'insecte *f* pee-kewr dahN-sect
insect spray spray anti-insectes *m* spreh ahN-tee aN-sekt
insoles semelles *f/pl* suh-mel
insulin insuline *f* aN-sew-leen

insured package colis à valeur déclarée *m* ko-lee ah vah-luhr day-klah-ray

intermission entracte *m* ahN-trahkt

internal interne aN-tehrn

international driver's license permis de conduire international *m* pehr-mee de kohN-dwee aN-tehr-nah-see-oh-nahl

internet internet *m*

internist spécialiste des maladies internes *m* spay-see-ah-leest day mah-lah-dee aN-tehrn

intersection croisement *m*, carrefour *m* krwahz-mahN, kah-foor

intestine les intestins *m/pl* lay-zaN-tes-taN

invalid pas valable pah vah-lah-bluh

to invite inviter aN-vee-teh

iodine iode *m* ee-awd

to iron repasser ruh-pahs-say

island île *f* eel

J

jack cric *m* kreek

jacket veste *f* vest

jacuzzi jacuzzi *m* zhah-kew-zee

jam confiture *f* kohN-fee-tewr

January janvier zhahN-vee-eh

jaw mâchoire *f* mah-shwahr

jeans jean *m* jean

jet ski scooter des mers *m* skoo-tuhr day mehr

jeweler's bijoutier *m* bee-zhoo-tyeh

jewelry bijoux *m/pl* bee-zhoo

Jewish juif zhweef

to jog faire du jogging fehr dew zhaw-ging

jogging jogging *m* zhaw-ging

joint articulation *f* ahr-tee-kew-lah-see-ohN

jug broc *m* brawk

juice jus *m* zhew

July juillet zhwee-eh

jumper cables câbles *m/pl* de démarrage kah-bluh duh day-mah-rahzh

June juin zhwaN

K

kayak kayak *m* kah-yahk

ketchup ketchup *m* ketch-up

key clé *f* klay

kidney rein *m* raN

kidney stones calculs *m/pl* rénaux kahl-kewl ray-noh

kilometer kilomètre *m* kee-low-meh-truh

king roi *m* rwah

kiosk kiosque *m* kee-awsk

kiwi kiwi *m* kee-vee

knee genou *m* zhen-oo

kneecap rotule *f* ro-tewl

knife couteau *m* koo-toh

L

lace dentelle *f* dahN-tel

lager beer bière *f* blonde bee-yehr blohNd

lake lac *m* lahk

lamb agneau *m* ahn-yo

lambswool mohair *m* mo-hehr

lamp lampe *f* lahNp

land excursion excursion *f* à terre ex-kewr-zee-ohN ah tehr

landing atterrissage *m* ah-tehr-ee-sahzh

landscape paysage *m* pay-ee-sahzh

226

Travel Dictionary

landslide éboulement *m* ay-bool-mahN

last name nom de famille *m* nohN duh fa-mee

last stop terminus *m* tehr-mee-newss

late tard tahr

later plus tard plew tahr

laundromat laverie automatique *f* lah-vuh-ree o-toh-mah-teek

laundry line corde à linge *f* kord ah laNzh

laundry room lavabos *m/pl* lah-vah-bo

lavender lavande *f* lah-vahNd

laxative laxatif *m* lahx-ah-teef

layers coupe en dégradé *f* koop ahN day-grah-day

leading role premier rôle *m* pruhm-yeh rawl

lean maigre meh-gruh

leather cuir *m* kweer

leather goods store maroquinerie *f* mah-raw-keen-uh-ree

leather sole semelle en cuir *f* suh-mel ahN kweer

to leave partir pah-teer

leek poireau *m* pwah-ro

left à gauche ah gohsh

leg jambe *f* zhahNb

lemon citron *m* see-trohN

lemonade limonade *f* lee-mo-nahd

lens objectif *m* awb-zhek-teef

lettuce salade *f* sah-lahd

library bibliothèque *f* bee-blee-o-tek

life jacket gilet de sauvetage *m* zhee-leh duh sohv-tahzh

life preserver bouée de sauvetage *f* boo-eh duh sohv-tahzh

lifeboat embarcation *f* de sauvetage ahN-bahr-kah-see-ohN duh sohv-tahzh

lift pass forfait de ski *m* for-feh duh ski

light lumière *f* lewm-yehr

light bulb ampoule *f* ahN-pool

lighter briquet *m* bree-keh

lightning éclair *m* ay-klehr

to like aimer em-eh

linen lin *m* laN

lip balm stick à lèvres *m* steek ah leh-vruh

lipstick rouge à lèvres *m* roozh ah leh-vruh

liver foie *m* fwah

liver pâté pâté de foie *m* pah-teh duh fwah

liverwurst saucisson *m* de campagne so-see-sohN duh kahN-pahn-yuh

lobby hall d'entrée *m* ahl dahN-treh

local time heure *f* locale uhr lo-kahl

local train RER *m* ehr-uh-ehr

locker consigne automatique *f* kohN-seen-yuh o-toh-mah-teek

logout annuler ah-new-lay

long long lohN

to lose perdre pehr-druh

lost and found bureau des objets trouvés *m* bew-ro day-zawb-zheh troo-veh

loud bruyant brew-yahN

lounge salle de réunion *f* sahl duh ray-ewn-yohN

low blood pressure tension, basse *f* tahN-see-ohN bahss

low tide marée basse *f* mah-ray bahss

low-pressure area dépression *f* day-pres-see-ohN

lower back pain lumbago *m* laN-bah-goh

lowfat milk lait demi-écrémé *m* lay duh-mee eh-kray-may
luggage bagages bah-gahzh
luggage car wagon à bagages *m* vah-gohN ah bah-gahzh
luggage counter enregistrement *m* des bagages ahN-reh-zhees-truh-mahN day bah-gahzh
luggage rack porte-bagages *m* pawt-bah-gahzh
luggage ticket bulletin d'enregistrement *m* bewl-taN dahN-reh-zhees-truh-mahN
lunch déjeuner *m* day-zhuh-nay
lungs *pl* les poumons *m/pl* lay poo-mohN

M

magazine magazine illustré *m* mah-gah-zeen ee-lew-stray
main course plat de résistance *m* plah duh ray-zees-tahNs
to make a date se donner rendez-vous suh dun-nay rahN-day-voo
to make reservations réserver ray-sehr-veh
malaria malaria *f* mahl-ah-ree-ah
man-made fiber synthétique *m* saN-teh-teek
marble marbre *m* mahr-bruh
March mars mahrss
margarine margarine *f* mah-gah-reen
market marché *m* mahr-shay
marmalade marmalade à l'orange *f* mahr-muh-lahd ah law-rahNzh
married marié mah-ree-eh
mascara rimmel *m* ree-mel
mask masque *m* mahsk

massage massage *m* mah-sahzh
matches les allumettes *f/pl* lay-zahl-ew-met
mattress matelas *m* maht-lah
mausoleum mausolée *m* mo-so-lay
May mai meh
mayonnaise mayonnaise *f* mah-yuh-nez
meal plat *m* plah
measles rougeole *f* roozh-awl
meat viande *f* vee-ahN
meat loaf steak *m* haché steak ahsh-eh
meditation méditation *f* may-dee-tah-see-ohN
to meet faire la connaissance de fehr lah koh-nay-sahNs duh
melon melon *m* muh-lohN
memorial site commémoratif *m* seet kohN-mem-or-ah-teef
meningitis méningite *f* may-nahN-geet
merengue meringue *f* mehr-aNg
microfiber microfibre *f* mee-kro-fee-bruh
Middle Ages *pl* moyen âge *m* mwah-yen ahzh
migraine migraine *f* mee-gren
mild doux doo
milk lait *m* lay
mill moulin *m* moo-laN
mineral water l'eau *f* minérale loh meen-eh-rahl
(non-sparkling) mineral water l'eau *f* minérale (non-gazeuse) loh meen-eh-rahl nohN-gah-zuhz
(sparkling) mineral water l'eau *f* minérale (gazeuse) loh meen-eh-rahl gah-zuhz
miniature golf course mini-golf *m* mee-nee gawlf

228

minibar minibar *m* mee-nee-bah

minute minute *f* meen-ewt

mirror miroir *m* meer-wahr

mixed grill grillade *f* gree-yahd

mixed salad salade *f* mixte sah-lahd meext

mixed vegetables macédoine *f* de légumes mah-seh-dwahn duh lay-gewm

mobility cane canne pour nonvoyants *f* kahn poor nohN-vwah-yahN

model maquette *f* mah-ket

modern moderne mo-dehrn

moisturizer crème de jour *f* krem duh zhoor

moisturizing mask masque hydratant *m* mahsk ee-drah-tahN

to molest importuner aN-pawr-tew-nay

monastery monastère *m* mohN-ah-stehr

Monday lundi laN-dee

money argent *m* ahr-zhahN

monkfish lotte *f* lawt

month mois *m* mwah

monument monument *m* mohN-ew-mahN

moon lune *f* lewn

morning matin *m* mah-taN

mosaic mosaïque *f* mo-zigh-eek

mosque mosquée *f* mos-kay

mosquito net moustiquaire *f* moos-tee-kehr

mosquito repellent protection anti-moustiques *f* pro-tek-see-ohN ahn-tee moo-steek

mother mère *f* mehr

motion sickness mal des voyages *m* mahl day vwah-ahzh

motorbike moto *f* moh-toh

motorboat bateau à moteur *m* bah-to ah mo-tuhr

mountain montagne *f* mohN-tahn-yuh

mountain climbing alpinisme *m* ahl-peen-eez-muh

mountain guide guide de montagne *m* geed duh mohN-tahn-yuh

mountain rescue service secours *m/pl* (en montagne) suh-koor (ahN mohN tahn-yuh)

mousse mousse coiffante *f* moos kwah-fahNt

moustache moustache *f* moo-stahsh

mouth bouche *f* boosh

movie theater cinéma *m* see-nay-mah

Mr. Monsieur muh-syuh

Ms. Madame *f* ma-dahm

mucus membrane muqueuse *f* mew-kuhz

mud mask boue *f* boo

mumps les oreillons *m/pl* lay-zor-eh-yohN

mural peinture murale *f* paN-tewr mew-rahl

muscle muscle *m* mews-kluh

museum musée *m* mew-zeh

mushrooms champignons *m/pl* shahN-peen-yohN

music musique *f* mew-zeek

music recital récital de chant *m* ray-see-tahl duh shahN

music store magasin de musique *m* mah-gah-zaN duh mew-zeek

musical comédie musicale *f* ko-may-dee mew-zee-kahl

muslim musulman *m* mew-sewl-mahN

mustard moutarde *f* moo-tahrd

mutton mouton *m* moo-tohN

229

N

nail file lime à ongles *f* leem ah ohN-gluh
nail polish vernis à ongles *m* vehr-nee ah ohN-gluh
nail polish remover dissolvant *m* dee-sawl-vahN
nail scissors *pl* ciseaux *m/pl* à ongles see-zo ah ohN-gluh
nailbrush brosse à ongles *f* brawss ah ohN-gluh
napkin serviette *f* sehr-vyet
narcotics drogue *f* drawg
national park parc national *m* pahrk nah-see-o-nahl
nationality nationalité *f* nah-see-oh-nahl-ee-teh
nationality sticker vignette de nationalité *f* veen-yet duh nah-see-oh-nah-ee-teh
natural fiber fibres *f/pl* naturelles fee-bruh nah-tewr-el
nature preserve site naturel protégé *m* seet nah-tew-rel pro-teh-zheh
nausea mal au cœur *m* mahl o kuhr
navy blue bleu marine (unv) bluh mah-reen
nearby près de preh duh
neck cou *m* koo
necklace chaîne *f* shen
nectarine nectarine *f* nek-tah-reen
negative négatif *m* nay-gah-teef
nerve nerf *m* nehr(f)
neuralgia névralgie *f* nev-rahl-zhee
neutral point mort *m* pwaN maw
newsstand marchand de journaux *m* mahr-shahN duh zhoor-no

230

next to à côté de ah ko-teh duh
next year année *f* prochaine ah-nay pro-shen
night nuit *f* nwee
night cream crème de nuit *f* krem duh nwee
nipple tétine *f* teh-teen
no-parking zone interdiction *f* de stationner aN-tehr-deek-see-ohN duh stah-see-ohN-nay
non-alcoholic beer bière *f* sans alcool bee-yehr sahN ahl-kawl
non-carbonated/still mineral water eau *f* minérale non gazeuse oh meen-eh-rahl nohN gah-zuhz
non-smoking non-fumeurs nohN few-muhr
non-swimmers non-nageur *m* nohN-nah-zhuhr
noodles pâtes *f/pl* paht
nose nez *m* nay
nose bleed saignements *m/pl* de nez sen-yuh-mahN duh nay
nose drops gouttes *f/pl* pour le nez goot poor luh nay
not far pas loin pah lwaN
novel roman *m* ro-mahN
November novembre no-vahN-bruh
now maintenant maN-tuh-nahN
nude beach plage naturiste *f* plahzh nah-tew-reest
number numéro *m* new-mehr-o
nuts noix *f/pl* nwah

O

obelisk obélisque *m* o-bel-eesk
observatory observatoire *m* awb-sehr-vah-twahr
occupation profession *f* pro-fes-syohN

ocean mer f mehr
October octobre aw-tawb-ruh
off-peak season basse saison f bahss say-sohN
oil huile f weel
oil change vidange f vee-dahNzh
ointment pommade f pum-ahd
olive oil huile f d'olive weel doh-leev
olives les olives f/pl lay-zo-leev
omelette omelette f awm-let
on sale article m en promotion ahr-tee-kluh ahN pro-mo-see-ohN
onion oignon m ohN-yohN
onion soup soupe f à l'oignon soop ah lohN-yohN
open ouvert oo-vehr
open-air theater théâtre de plein air m teh-ah-truh duh plen air
opening night première f pruhm-yehr
opera opéra m o-peh-rah
opera house Opéra m o-pehr-ah
operetta opérette f oh-peh-ret
opposite en face de ahN fahss duh
optician opticien m awp-tee-see-aN
oral oral aw-rahl
orange orange f aw-rahNzh
orange juice jus d'orange m zhew daw-rahNzh
orchestra orchestre m aw-kes-truh
orchestra (seating) parterre m pah-tehr
to order commander kohN-mahN-day
oregano origan m aw-ree-gahn
organ orgue m awrg
original original m o-ree-zhee-nahl

original version version originale f vehr-zee-ohN o-ree-zhee-nahl
orthopedist orthopédiste m or-toh-pay-deest
outbox messages m/pl envoyés mes-sahzh ahN-vwah-yeh
outlet prise (de courant) f preez duh koo-rahN
oven-browned gratiné grah-tee-nay
oysters huîtres f/pl weet-ruh

P

pacemaker pacemaker m pace-make-ehr
pacifier sucette f sew-set
pack compresse f kohN-press
painkiller analgésique m ahn-ahl-zheh-seek
painter peintre m paN-truh
painting peinture f paN-tewr
pajamas pl pyjama m pee-dzhah-mah
palace palais m pah-leh
panorama panorama m pah-naw-rah-mah
panties pl culotte f kew-lawt
pants pl pantalon m pahN-tah-lohN
pantyhose collant m ko-lahN
paper papier m pahp-yeh
paper towels rouleau de papier (absorbant) m roo-lo duh pah-pyeh ahb-sawr-bahN
paprika piment m pee-mahN
paragliding parapente m pah-rah-pahNt
paraplegic paraplégique pah-rah-play-zheek
to park se garer suh gah-ray
park parc m pahrk

231

parking disc disque horaire
deesk oh-rehr

parking lot parking *m* pahr-
king

parking meter parcmètre *m*
pahrk-meh-truh

parsley persil *m* pehr-see

partner compagnon *m* /
compagne *f* kohN-pahn-
yohN/kohN-pahn-yuh

passport passeport *m*
pahss-por

pasta pâtes *f/pl* paht

pastries gâteaux *m/pl* secs
gah-toh sek

pastry shop pâtisserie *f*
pah-tee-suh-ree

path chemin *m* shuh-maN

to pay payer pay-yeh

to pay duty payer le droit de
douane pay-eh luh dwah duh
dwahn

to pay separately payer,
séparément pay-eh say-pahr-
eh-mahN

to pay together payer,
ensemble pay-yeh ahN-sahN-
bluh

peach pêche *f* pehsh

peak season haute saison *f*
oht say-sohN

peanuts cacahuètes *f/pl* kah-
kah-wet

pear poire *f* pwahr

pearl perle *m* pehrl

peas petits pois *m/pl*
puh-tee pwah

pedal boat pédalo *m*
pay-dah-lo

pedestrian zone zone
piétonne *f* zohn pyeh-tun

pediatrician pédiatre *m* pay-
dee-ah-truh

peeling peeling *m* pee-ling

pelvis bassin *m* bah-saN

pencil crayon *m* kray-ohN

pencil sharpener taille-crayon
m tigh-kray-ohN

pendant pendentif *m*
pahN-dahN-teef

peninsula péninsule *f*
pa-naN-sewl

(ground) pepper poivre *m*
pwahv-ruh

pepper steak steak *m* au
poivre steak oh pwahv-ruh

pepperoni salami *m*
sah-lah-mee

perfume parfum *m* pahr-faN

perfume shop parfumerie *f*
pah-few-muh-ree

periodontal disease
parodontose *f* pah-rah-dohN-
toh-zuh

periods *pl* menstruations *f/pl*
mahN-strew-ah-see-ohN

pharmacy pharmacie *f*
fahr-mah-see

phone telephone *m*
tel-eh-fohn

photo photo *f* fo-toh

photo shop magasin d'articles
photographiques *m* mah-
gah-zaN dahr-tee-kluh fo-toh-
grah-feek

physician médecin généraliste
m made-saN zhehn-nehr-ah-
leest

pickles cornichons *m/pl*
kaw-nee-shohN

pickpocket pickpocket *m*
peek-paw-ket

picture tableau *m* tah-blo

picture book livre d'images
pour enfants *m* lee-vruh dee-
mahzh poor ahN-fahN

piece morceau *m* maw-so

pig's feet pieds *m/pl* de cochon
pee-yeh duh ko-shohN

pike brochet *m* braw-sheh

pillar colonne *f* ko-lun

pillow oreiller *m* o-ray-eh

232

pilot pilote *m* pee-lote
PIN code secret *m*
  code suh-keeh
pineapple ananas *m*
  ah-nah-nah
pink rose rohz
pipe pipe *f* peep
pipe cleaner cure-pipe *m*
  kewr-peep
pizza pizza *f* peets-ah
plain omelette omelette *f*
  nature awm-let nah-tewr
plane avion *m* ah-vee-ohN
planetarium planétarium *m*
  plahn-eh-tah-ree-um
plastic cup gobelet en
  plastique *m* gawb-lay ahN
  plah-steek
plastic plate assiette *f* en
  plastique ahs-syet ahN plah-
  steek
plastic untensils couverts *m/pl*
  en plastique koo-vehr ahN
  plah-steek
plastic wrap film fraîcheur *m*
  feelm freh-shuhr
plate assiette *f* ah-syet
platform quai *m* keh
to the platforms accès aux
  quais ahk-seh oh keh
platinum platine *f* plah-teen
to play jouer zhoo-eh
play pièce de théâtre *f* pee-yes
  duh teh-ah-truh
playground terrain de jeux *m*
  tehr-aN duh zhuh
playing cards cartes *f/pl* à jouer
  kahrt ah zhoo-eh
playpen parc *m* pahrk
please s'il vous plaît
  see voo-play
pliers pince *f* pahNss
plug fiche *f* feesh
plums prunes *f/pl* prewn
pneumonia pneumonie *f*
  pnuh-mun-ee

poached trout truite *f* au bleu
  trweet oh bluh
pocket calculator calculette *f*
  kahl-kew-let
pocket knife couteau de poche
  m koo-toh duh pawsh
poles bâtons *m/pl* de ski
  bah-tohN duh ski
police police *f* poo-leess
policeman gendarme *m*
  zhahN-dahrm
polio poliomyélite *f*
  paw-lee-um-yeh-leet
polluted pollué paw-lew-eh
pop concert concert pop *m*
  kohN-sehr pawp
porcelain filling plombage en
  porcelaine *m* plohN-bahzh
  ahN pawr-suh-len
pork porc *m* pawr
pork chops côte *f* kawt
port porto *m* paw-toh
portion portion *f* paw-see-ohN
portrait portrait *m* pawr-treh
postcard carte postale *f*
  kahrt pos-tahl
poster poster *m* paws-tehr
pot roast bœuf *m* mode
  buhf mode
potatoes pommes *f/pl* de terre
  pum duh tehr
pottery poterie *f* paw-teh-ree
pottery, ceramics céramique *f*
  seh-rah-meek
poultry volaille *f* vol-igh-yuh
powder poudre *f* poo-druh
precipitation précipitations *f/pl*
  pray-see-pee-tah-see-ohN
pregnant women femmes
  enceintes fahm ahN-saNt
prescription ordonnance *f*
  aw-dun-ahNs
print imprimer aN-pree-may
printer cartridge cartouche
  d'imprimante *f* kahr-toosh
  daN-pree-mahNt

production mise en scène f
meez-ahN sen

program programme m
pro-grahm

property management gestion
f zhes-teeohN

protestant protestant m
pro-tes-tahN

pulled ligament entorse f
ahN-tors

pulled muscle claquage
musculaire m klah-kahzh
mews-cew-lehr

pulled tendon élongation f
ay-lohN-gah-see-ohN

pump pompe à air f
pohNp ah ehr

pure new wool pure
laine vierge f pewr len
vee-yerzh

purification épuration f ay-
pew-rah-see-ohN

purple violet vee-o-lay

purse, handbag sac à main m
sahk ah maN

Q

queen reine f ren

R

radiator radiateur m
rah-dee-ah-tuhr

radio radio f rah-dyo

(rubber) raft bateau
pneumatique m bah-to pnuh-
mah-teek

raincoat imperméable m
aN-pehr-may-ah-bluh

rainy pluvieux plew-vyuh

ramp voie d'accès à
l'autoroute f vwah dahk-say
ah lo-tow-root

234

range cuisinière f
kwee-seen-yehr

rash éruption f cutanée
ay-rewp-see-ohN kew-tahn-eh

raspberries framboises f/pl
frahN-bwahz

ravine gorges f/pl gawrz

raw cru krew

razor rasoir m rah-swah

razor blade lame de rasoir m
lahm duh rah-swah

rear mezzanine deuxième
balcon m duh-zee-em bahl-
kohN

rear-end collision télescopage
m teh-leh-skoh-pahzh

rear-view mirror rétroviseur m
ray-tro-vee-suhr

receipt reçu m ray-sew

recently il y a peu de temps
eel yah puh duh tahN

reception réception f
ray-sep-see-ohN

rectal rectal rek-tahl

red rouge roozh

red cabbage chou m rouge
shoo roozh

red wine vin rouge m
vaN roozh

referee arbitre m ahr-bee-truh

reflexology massage massage
des zones de réflexe du pied
m mah-sahzh day zohn duh
ray-flex dew pyeh

refrigerator réfrigérateur m
ray-free-zheh-ah-tuhr

regatta régate f ray-gaht

relief relief m ruh-lyef

religion religion f reh-lee-zhee-
yohN

remains vestiges m/pl
ves-teezh

renaissance Renaissance f
ruh-nay-sahNs

rent loyer m lwah-yeh

to rent louer loo-eh

rental fee prix de la location *m* pree duh lah lo-kah-see-ohN
repair réparation *f* ray-pah-rah-see-ohN
to repair réparer ray-pah-ray
to repeat répéter ray-pay-teh
to replace changer shahN-zheh
reply réponse *f* ray-pohNs
reply all répondre à tous ray-pohN-druh ah toos
reserved réservé ray-zehr-veh
reservoir lac artificiel *m* lahk ahr-tee-fee-see-el
restaurant restaurant *m* rest-o-rahN
restored restauré res-toh-ray
restrooms toilettes twah-let
to return rendre rahN-druh
return flight vol de retour *m* vol duh ruh-tour
rheumatism rhumatisme *m* ree-mah-teez-muh
rib côte *f* kawt
rice riz *m* ree
to ride (horseback) faire du cheval fehr dew shuh-vahl
right à droite ah drwaht
right of way priorité *f* pree-aw-ree-teh
ring bague *f* bahg
river rivière *f* ree-vyehr
river rafting rafting *m* rahf-ting
road route *f* root
road map carte routière *f* kahrt roo-tyehr
roast rôti *m* ro-tee
roasted rôti ro-tee
rock concert concert rock *m* kohN-sehr rawk
rock lobster langouste *f* lahN-goost
roll petit pain *m* puh-tee paN
rolled oats flocons *m/pl* d'avoine flaw-kohN dah-vwahn

Roman romain ro-maN
Romanesque roman ro-mahN-esk
Romantic romantique ro-mahN-teek
room chambre *f* shahN-bruh
root racine *f* rah-seen
root canal traitement de la racine *m* tret-mahN duh lah rah-seen
rope corde *f* kawrd
rosemary romarin *m* ro-mah-raN
rosé wine vin *m* rosé vaN ro-zeh
rough seas *pl.* mer agitée *f* mehr ah-zhee-teh
row rang *m* rahN
row boat bateau à rames *m* bah-to ah rahm
rubber boots bottes *f/pl* en caoutchouc bawt ahN kah-oo-tshoo
ruins *pl* ruines *f/pl* rew-een
RV (recreational vehicle) camping-car *m* kahN-ping kah

S

saddle selle *f* sel
saddlebags sacoches *f/pl* sah-kawsh
safe coffre-fort *m* kawf-ruh for
safety pin épingle *f* de sûreté ay-paN-gluh duh sewr-teh
to sail faire de la voile fehr duh lah vwahl
sail boat voilier *m* vwahl-yeh
salad salade *f* sah-lahd
sale soldes *f/pl* sawld
salmon saumon *m* so-mohN
salt sel *m* sel
sand sable *m* sah-bluh
sandals sandales *f/pl* sahN-dahl

235

sandpaper papier émeri *m* pahp-yeh ehm-ree

sandstone grès *m* greh

sandwich sandwich *m* sahN-dweetch

sandy beach plage de sable *m* plahzh duh sah-bluh

sanitary napkins serviettes *f/pl* hygiéniques sehrv-yet hee-zhen-eek

sarcophagus sarcophage *m* sahr-ko-fahzh

Saturday samedi sahm-dee

sauce sauce *f* sohss

saucepan casserole *f* kahss-rawl

sauerkraut choucroute *f* shoo-kroot

sauna sauna *m* so-nah

sausages saucisse *f* so-seess

save sauvegarder sohv-gahr-day

savings bank caisse d'épargne *f* kess day-pahr-nyuh

scallops coquilles *f/pl* Saint-Jacques ko-kee saN-zhahk

scampi angoustines *f/pl* ahN-goos-teen

scarf écharpe *f* ay-shahrp

schedule horaire *m* o-rehr

school école *f* ay-kuhl

sciatica sciatique *f* syah-teek

scissors *pl* ciseaux *m/pl* see-zo

scrambled eggs œuf *m* brouillé uhf broo-yeh

screw vis *f* veess

screwdriver tournevis *m* toor-nuh veess

sculptor sculpteur *m* skewlp-tuhr

sculpture sculpture *f* skewlp-tewr

sea urchin oursin *m* oor-saN

seafood platter plateau *m* de fruits de mer plah-toh duh frwee duh mehr

seasoned assaisonné ah-say-zohN-nay

seat place *f* plahss

seatbelt ceinture de sécurité *f* saN-tewr duh say-kew-ree-teh

second seconde *f* suh-kohNd

self-service libre service *m* lee-bruh sehr-veess

self-timer déclencheur automatique *m* day-klahN-shuhr o-toh-mah-teek

semolina semoule *f* suh-mool

send envoyer ahN-vwah-yeh

to send envoyer ahN-vwah-yeh

sender expéditeur *m* ex-pay-dee-tuhr

sent mails messages *m/pl* envoyés mess-ahzh ahN-vwah-yeh

September septembre sep-tahN-bruh

service service *m* sehr-veess

service area relais routier *m* ruh-lay roo-tyeh

sewing needle aiguille *f* à coudre ay-gwee ah koo-druh

sewing thread fil à coudre *m* feel ah koo-druh

sexually transmitted disease (STD) maladie vénérienne *f* mah-lah-dee veh-nay-ree-en

shade ombre *f* ohN-bruh

shampoo shampooing *m* shahN-pwaN

to shave raser rah-zeh

shaving cream mousse à raser *f* mooss ah rah-zeh

sheet drap *m* drah

shells coquillages *m/pl* ko-kee-yahzh

shelter refuge *m* ruh-fewzh

shinbone tibia *m* tee-bee-ah

ship bateau *m* bah-toh

ship's doctor médecin de bord *m* med-saN duh bohr

shirt chemise *f* shmeez

shock choc *m* shawk
shock absorber amortisseur *m* ah-maw-teess-suhr
shoe polish cirage *m* see-rahzh
shoe repair shop cordonnier *m* kaw-dohN-yeh
shoe store magasin de chaussures *m* mah-gah-zaN duh sho-sewr
shoelaces lacets *m/pl* lah-say
shoes chaussures *f/pl* sho-sewr
shopping center centre commercial *m* sahN-truh kohN-mehr-see-ahl
short court koor
short sleeves manches courtes *f/pl* mahNsh koort
shorts short *m* shawr
shoulder épaule *f* ay-pohl
to show montrer mohN-tray
shower douche *f* doosh
shower gel gel douche *m* zhel doosh
shrimp, prawn crevette *f* kruh-vet
shuttlecock volant *m* vo-lahN
sick bag sachet en cas de nausée *m* sah-sheh ahN kah duh no-zeh
side dish garniture *f* gahr-nee-tewr
side effects effets secondaires eh-feh suh-kohN-dehr
sights curiosités *f/pl* kew-ree-aws-see-teh
sightseeing tour excursion *f* ex-kewr-zee-ohN
signature signature *f* seen-ya-tewr
silk soie *f* swah
silk scarf foulard en soie *m* foo-lahr ahN swah
silver argent *m* ah-zhahN
silverware couverts *m/pl* koo-vehr
since depuis duh-pwee

singer chanteur *m* / chanteuse *f* shahN-tuhr/shahN-tuhz
single simple *m* saN-pluh
single bed lit à une place *m* lee ah ewn plahss
sink lavabo *m* lah-vah-bo
sinus sinus *m* see-newss
sister sœur suhr
size pointure *f* pwaN-tewr
ski ski *m* ski
ski mask lunettes *f/pl* de ski lew-net duh ski
skiing instructor moniteur de ski *m* mun-ee-tuhr duh ski
skiing wax fart *m* fahr
skin peau *f* po
skin diagnosis diagnostic du type de peau *m* dee-ahg-naws-teek dew teep duh po
skirt jupe *f* jewp
skydiving saut en parachute *m* soht ahN pah-rah-shewt
sleeper car wagon-lit *m* vah-gohN-lee
sleeping bag sac de couchage *m* sahk duh koo-shahzh
sleeping pills somnifères *m/pl* sum-nee-fehr
slowly lentement lahN-tuh-mahN
SLR camera réflex *m* ray-flex
smog smog *m* smawg
smoked fumé few-may
smoked ham jambon *m* fumé zhaN-bohN few-may
smoked salmon saumon *m* fumé so-mohN few-may
smoking fumeurs few-muhr
snails escargots *m/pl* es-kahr-go
sneakers baskets *m/pl* bahs-keht
snorkel tube de plongée *m* tewb duh plohN-zheh
snow neige *m* nehzh

237

snow chains chaînes f/pl
à neige shen ah nehzh
soap savon m sah-vohN
soccer ball football m
fooht-bahl
soccer field terrain de football
m tehr-raN duh fooht-bahl
soccer game match de football
m mahtch duh fooht-bahl
socks chaussettes f/pl sho-set
soda limonade f lee-mo-nahd
sold out complet kohN-pleh
sole sole f sawl
solid-color uni ew-nee
soloist soliste m/soliste f
so-leest/so-leest
something for ... le remède
contre ... luh ruh-may-duh
kohN-truh
sometimes quelquefois
kel-kuh-fwah
son fils m feess
soon bientôt bee-aN-toe
soup potage m po-tahzh
sour aigre eh-gruh
souvenir souvenir m soo-ven-
eer
souvenir shop magasin de
souvenirs m mah-gah-saN duh
soo-ven-eer
spare part pièce de rechange f
pee-ess duh ruh-shahNzh
spare tire roue de secours f
roo duh suh-koor
spark plug bougie f
boo-zhee
sparkling wine vin m
mousseux vaN moos-suh
sparkling mineral water eau f
minérale gazeuse
o meen-eh-rahl gah-zuhz
to speak parler pah-lay
specialty spécialité f
speh-see-ah-lee-teh
(film) speed sensibilité f
saN-see-bee-lee-teh

speedometer compteur de
vitesse m kohN-tuhr duh vee-
tess
spices les épices f/pl
lay-zeh-peess
spinach les épinards m/pl
lay-zeh-pee-nahr
spine colonne vertébrale f
ko-lun vehr-teh-brahl
spirits eau-de-vie f
oh-duh-vee
spoon cuillère f kwee-yehr
sporting goods store magasin
d'articles de sport m mah-
gah-zaN dahr-tee-kluh duh
spawr
sports jacket veston m
ves-tohN
sprained foulé foo-lay
spring printemps m praN-tahN
square place f plahss
squash squash m squash
squash ball balle de squash f
bahl duh squash
squash racket raquette de
squash f rah-ket duh squash
stadium stade m stahd
stain remover détachant m
day-tahsh-mahN
stamp timbre(-poste) m
taN-bruh pawst
standing room ticket place
debout f plahss duh-boo
star étoile f ay-twahl
start of the season avant-
saison f ah-vahN say-zohN
starter démarreur m
day-mah-ruhr
stationery store papeterie f
pahp-eh-tree
statue statue f stah-tew
steak bifteck m beef-tek
steam bath bain de vapeur m
baN duh vah-puhr
steamed (cuit) à la vapeur
kwee ah lah vah-puhr

steamed (food) à l'étuvé ah lay-tew-veh
steering direction f dee-rek-see-ohN
steward steward m stew-ahr
sting piqûre f pee-kewr
stockings mi-bas m/pl mee-bah
stolen volé vaw-lay
stomach estomac m ess–toh-mah
stomach ache maux m/pl d'estomac mo day-stoh-mah
stomach ulcer ulcère m à l'estomac ewl-sehr ah les-toh-mah
stoneware faïence f figh-yahNs
stop arrêt m ah-ray
to stop s'arrêter sah-reh-teh
stopover escale f es-kahl
storm tempête f tahN-pet
storm warning avis m de tempête ah-vee duh tahN-pet
stormy orageux o-rahzh-uh
stove réchaud m ray-sho
straight ahead tout droit too dwah
strawberries fraises f/pl frehz
strawberry ice cram glace f à la fraise glahss ah la frehz
street rue f rew
stroke attaque f (d'apoplexie) ah-tahk dah-po-plex-ee
stroller poussette f poo-set
student étudiant m/ étudiante f ay-tew-dyahN/ay-tew-dyahNt
to study faire des études fehr day-zeh-tewd
style style m steel
styling gel gel coiffant m zhel kwah-fahN
subtitle sous-titres m/pl soo-tee-truh
suede chamois m shah-mwah
sugar sucre m sew-kruh
suit (for men) costume m kaw-stewm

suit (for women) tailleur m ta-yuhr
suitable for the disabled (aménagé) pour les handi-capés ah-men-ah-zheh poor lay ahN-dee-kah-pay
suitcase valise f vah-leez
summer été m ay-teh
summit sommet m sum-may
sun soleil m so-lay
sun protection factor (SPF) facteur de protection solaire m fahk-tuhr duh pro-tek-see-ohN so-lehr
sunburn coup de soleil m koo duh so-lay
Sunday dimanche dee-mahNsh
sunglasses pl lunettes f/pl de soleil lewn-et duh so-lay
sunny ensoleillé ahN-so-leh-yeh
sunrise lever du soleil m leh-veh dew so-lay
sunroof toit ouvrant m twah oov-rahN
sunscreen crème solaire f krem so-lehr
sunset coucher du soleil m koo-shay dew so-lay
sunstroke insolation f aN-so-lah-see-ohN
suntan lotion lait solaire m lay so-lehr
supermarket supermarché m sew-pehr-mahr-sheh
suppository suppositoire m sew-paw-zee-twahr
surcharge supplément m sewp-pleh-mahN
surfboard planche à voile f plahNsh ah vwahl
surroundings pl les environs m/pl lay-zahN-vee-rohN
sweater pullover m pewl-oh-vehr
sweet sucré sew-kray

sweetbread ris *m* de veau
ree duh vo

sweetener saccharine *f*
sahk-ah-reen

swelling enflure *f* ahN-flewr

to swim se baigner
suh ben-yeh

to swim nager nah-zheh

swimming area plage gardée *f*
plahzh gahr-day

swimming pool piscine *f*
pee-seen

swimming trunks *pl* caleçon de
bain *m* kahl-sohN duh baN

switch guichet *m* ghee-sheh

synagogue synagogue *f*
see-nah-gawg

T

T-shirt T-shirt *m* tee shert

table table *f* tah-bluh

table tennis ping-pong *m*
ping-pohN

table wine vin *m* de pays
vaN duh pay-ee

table wine vin *m* de table
vaN duh tah-bluh

tablecloth nappe *f* nahp

tablets comprimés kohN-pree-
may

tail light feux *m/pl* arrière
fuh ah-ree-ehr

to take photographs prendre
des photos pahN-druh day
fo-toh

taken occupé o-kew-pay

tampons tampons *m/pl*
tahN-pohN

tanning salon solarium *m*
so-lah-ree-um

tape ruban adhésif *m*
rew-bahN ahd-eh-seef

tarragon estragon *m*
ess-trah-gohN

tartar tartre tahr-truh

to taste être bon et-ruh bohN

taxi stand station de taxis
stah-see-ohN duh tahx-ee

tea thé *m* teh

teabag sachet de thé *m*
sah-sheh duh teh

team équipe *f* ay-keep

telephoto lens téléobjectif *m*
teh-lay-awb-zhek-teef

temperature température *f*
tahN-pehr-ah-tewr

temple temple *m* tahN-pluh

temporary filling traitement
provisoire *m* tret-mahN
pro-vee-zwahr

tendon tendon *m* than-dohN

tennis tennis *m* ten-eess

tennis ball balle de tennis *f*
bahl duh ten-eess

tennis racket raquette de
tennis *f* rah-ket duh ten-eess

tent tente *f* tahNt

tent peg piquet (de tente) *m*
pee-keh duh tahNt

terrace terrasse *f* teh-rahss

terracotta terre cuite *f*
tehr kweet

tetanus tétanos *m*
teh-tahn-oss

thank you merci mehr-see

theater théâtre *m* teh-ah-truh

there là-bas lah bah

thermal current courant
ascensionnel *m* koo-rahN-tah-
sahN-see-o-nel

thermal spa bain thermal *m*
baN tehr-mahl

thermometer thermomètre
médical *m*
tehr-mo-meh-truh

thermos thermos *m*
tehr-mawss

thief voleur *m* vol-uhr

three trois trwah

throat gorge *f* gawrzh

throat drops cachets *m/pl* pour la gorge kah-shay poor luh gawrzh

thunder tonnerre *m* tun-ehr

thunderstorm orage *m* o-rahzh

Thursday jeudi zhuh-dee

thyme thym *m* taN

thyroid gland thyroïde *f* teer-aw-eed

tick bite piqûre de tique *f* pee-kewr duh teek

ticket billet *m* bee-yeh

ticket (subway) ticket *m* tee-keh

ticket machine distributeur automatique de tickets *m* deess-tree-bew-tuhr oh-toh-mah-teek duh tee-keh

ticket validation machine composteur *m* kohN-paws-tuhr

tie cravate *f* krah-vaht

(a) tie match nul mahtch newl

tight serré sehr-ray

time temps *m* tahN

tip pourboire *m* poor-bwahr

tire pneu *m* puh-nuh

tire pressure pression des pneus *f* pres-see-ohN

tissues disques *m/pl* à démaquiller deesk ah day-mah-kee-eh

tissues mouchoirs *m/pl* en papier moosh-wahr ahN pah-pyeh

tobacconist bureau de tabac *m* bew-ro duh tah-bah

toboggan run piste de luge *f* peest duh lewzh

today aujourd'hui oh-zhoor-dwee

toe orteil *m* or-teh

toilet paper papier hygiénique *m* pah-pyeh hee-zhen-eek

toilet/restroom toilettes *f/pl* twah-let

toll péage *m* pay-ahzh

tomato tomate *f* toh-maht

tomato juice jus *m* de tomate zhew duh toh-maht

tomato salad salade *f* de tomates sah-lahd duh toh-maht

tomorrow demain duh-maN

tongue langue *f* lahNg

tonight ce soir suh swahr

tonsillitis angine *f* ahN-zheen

tonsils les amygdales *f/pl* lay-zah-mee-dahl

tools outils *m/pl* oo-tee

tooth dent *f* dahN

toothbrush brosse à dents *f* brawss ah dahN

toothpaste dentifrice *m* dahN-tee-freess

toothpick cure-dents *m* kewr-dahN

torn ligament déchirure des ligaments *f* day-shee-rewr day lee-gah-mahN

tour boat vedette d'excursion *f* veh-det dek-skewr-zee-ohN

tour group groupe (de touristes) *m* group duh toor-eest

tourist guide guide *m* gheed

tourist office syndicat d'initiative *m* saN-dee-kah dee-nee-see-ah-teev

tow rope câble de remorquage *m* kah-bluh duh ruh-maw-kahzh

tow truck dépanneuse *f* day-pahn-nuhz

towel serviette *f* sehr-vee-et

tower tour *f* toor

town ville *f* veel

town center centre-ville *m* sahN-truh veel

town gate porte de la ville *f* pawt duh lah veel

town hall hôtel *m* de ville
o-tel duh veel

town wall remparts *m/pl*
rahN-pahr

toy jouet *m* zhoo-eh

track voie vwah

track pants *pl* pantalon de
jogging *m* pahN-tah-lohN duh
zhaw-ging

tracksuit tenue de jogging *f*
tuh-new duh zhawg-ing

traffic lights feu *m* fuh

trail piste de ski de fond *f*
peest duh ski duh fohN

trailer caravane *f*
kah-rah-vahn

train train *m* traN

train station gare *f* gahr

tranquilizer calmant *m*
kahl-mahN

to transfer changer de train
shahN-zheh duh traN

transfer virement *m*
veer-mahN

transmission boîte de vitesses
f bwaht duh vee-tess

trash corbeille *f* kaw-bay

travel bag sac de voyage *m*
sahk duh vwah-yahzh

travel guide guide de voyage
m geed duh vwah-ahzh

treasury trésor *m* treh-sawr

trip traversée *f* tah-vehr-say

trout truite *f* trweet

Tuesday mardi mahr-dee

tuna thon *m* tohN

turbot turbot *m* tew-boh

turnips navets *m/pl* nah-veh

turquoise turquoise tewr-
kwahz

TV télévision *f* teh-lay-vee-see-
ohN

TV room salle de télévision *f*
sahl duh teh-lay-vee-see-ohN

tweezers *pl* pince à épiler *f*
paNs ah eh-pee-lay

242

ulcer ulcère ewl-sehr

umpire arbitre *m*
ah-bee-truh

uncooked ham jambon *m*
cru zhaN-bohN krew

undershirt maillot de corps *m*
mah-yoh duh kawr

to understand comprendre
kohN-prahN-druh

underwear dessous *m/pl*
duh-soo

university université *f*
ewn-ee-vehr-see-teh

until jusqu'à zhews-kah

up the steps en haut de
l'escalier ahN-noh duh les-
kahl-yeh

urologist urologue *m*
ew-ro-lawg

UV filter filtre UV *m*
feel-truh ew-veh

vacation vacances *f/pl* vah-
kahNs

vacation apartment/rental
meublé *m* muh-blay

vacation home maison de
vacances *f* may-sohN duh vah-
kahNs

vaccination card carnet
de vaccinations *m*
kahr-neh duh vahk-see-nah-see-
ohN

valid valable vah-lah-bluh

to validate composter
kohN-paws-teh

valley vallée *f* vah-lay

valve valve *f* vahlv

vanilla ice cream glace *f* à la
vanille glahss ah lah vah-nee-
yuh

variable capricieux
  kah-pree-see-uh
variety show variétés f/pl
  vah-ree-eh-teh
vase vase m vahz
VAT (value added tax) TVA f
  teh-veh-ah
vault voûte f voot
veal veau m vo
veal filet escalope f
  ess-kah-lawp
vegetables légumes m/pl
  lay-gewm
vegetarian végétarien
  veh-zheh-tah-ree-aN
vehicle documents
  papiers m/pl
  de la voiture pah-pyeh duh
  lah vwah-tewr
vehicle registration carte grise
  m kahrt greez
venison cerf m sehr
verbena tea infusion f
  de verveine an-few-zee-ohN
  duh vehr-ven
vertebrae vertèbre f
  vehr-teb-ruh
vest gilet m zhee-lay
veterinarian vétérinaire m
  veh-teh-ree-nehr
victory victoire f
  veek-twahr
video camera caméra vidéo f
  kahm-eh-rah vee-day-o
video cassette vidéocassette f
  vee-day-o-kah-set
view vue f vew
vinegar vinaigre m
  vee-nehg-ruh
to visit visiter vee-zee-teh
volleyball volley m
  vol-lay
voltage voltage m
  vol-tahzh
vomiting vomissements m/pl
  vaw-meess-mahN

W

to wait attendre ah-tahn-druh
waiting room salle d'attente
  sahl dah-tahNt
walking shoes chaussures f/pl
  de randonnée sho-sewr duh
  rahN-dun-eh
walking stick cannes f/pl kahn
walkman® baladeur m
  bah-lah-duhr
wall mur m mewr
wallet portefeuille m pawt-
  fuh-yuh
wardrobe armoire f ahr-mwahr
to wash faire un shampooing
  fehr aN shahN-pwahN
washcloth gant de toilette m
  gahN duh twah-let
washing machine machine à
  laver f mah-sheen ah lah-veh
watch montre f mohN-truh
watch shop horloger aw-lo-
  zheh
watchband bracelet de montre
  m brahss-lay duh mohN-truh
water eau f o
water quality qualité de l'eau
  f kahl-ee-teh duh lo
water ski ski nautique m ski
  no-teek
watercolor aquarelle f ah-
  kwah-rel
waterfall cascade f kas-kahd
watermelon pastèque f
  pahss-tek
wave vague f vahg
wave pool piscine à vagues f
  pee-seen ah vahg
Wednesday mercredi
  mehr-kruh-dee
week semaine f suh-men
well-done bien cuit bee-aN
  kwee
wet mouillé moo-yeh
wheel roue f roo

wheel brace clef en croix *m* klay aN krwah

wheelchair lift plate-forme élévatrice *f* plaht-form eh-lay-vah-treess

white blanc, *m* blanche, *f* blahN blahnsh

white bread pain blanc *m* paN blahN

white wine vin blanc *m* vaN blahN

whole grain bread pain complet *m* paN kohN-pleh

whooping cough coqueluche *f* kaw-kel-ewsh

wide-angle lens objectif *m* grand angle awb-zhek-teef grahn-than-gluh

wife femme *f* fahm

wild boar sanglier *m* sahN-glee-eh

wild hare lièvre *m* lee-eh-vruh

to win gagner gahn-yeh

wind vent *m* vahN

window fenêtre *f* fuh-net-ruh

window display vitrine *f* vee-treen

windshield wipers essuie-glace *m* ess-wee glahss

wine vin *m* vaN

winter hiver *m* ee-vehr

wiper blades balais *m/pl* d'essuie-glace bah-lay dess-wee-glahss

wire fil métallique *m* feel may-tah-leek

wisdom tooth dent de sagesse *f* dahN duh sah-zhess

witness témoin *m* teh-mwahN

wool laine *f* len

works œuvre *f* uh-vruh

wound blessure *f* bles-sewr

wrench clef à écrous *f* klay ah eh-kroo

wrinkle-free infroissable aN-frwah-sah-bluh

writing pad bloc-notes *m* blawk-noht

writing paper papier à lettres *m* pahp-yeh ah leh-truh

Y

year année *f* ah-nay

yellow jaune zhone

yesterday hier yehr

yoga yoga *m* yo-gah

yogurt yaourt *m* yah-oor

youth hostel auberge *f* de jeunesse o-behrzh duh zhuh-ness

youth hostel ID carte d'adhérent des auberges de jeunesse *f* kahrt dah-dehr-rahN day-zo-behrzh duh zhuh-ness

Z

zip code code postal *m* code paws-tahl

zipper fermeture éclaire *f* fehr-meh-tewr eh-klehr

zoo zoo *m* zo

zoom lens zoom *m* zoom

zucchini courgette *f* koor-zhet

Signs

A

accès *m* access; **Accès interdit!** No access!
accueil *m* reception
adresse *f* address
à droite right
adultes *m/pl* adults
aéroport *m* airport
à gauche left
agence *f* agency; **– de voyage** travel agency
aire *f* **de repos** highway rest area
alimentation *f* grocery store
Allô! Hello! *(on the phone)*
à louer for rent
ambulance *f* ambulance
anglais English
à midi at noon
Appuyez! Push!
après-midi *m* afternoon
arrêt *m* (bus/subway) stop
arrivée *f* arrival
ascenseur *m* elevator; lift
Attention! Attention! / Watch out!
autobus *m* bus
autorisé permitted
autoroute *f* express way
Au revoir! Good bye!
Au secours! Help!
à vendre for sale

B

barré closed-off
Belgique *f* Belgium
Bienvenue! Welcome!
billet *m* money bill; ticket
boissons *f/pl* beverages
boîte *f* **aux lettres** mail box

boucherie *f* butcher's
boulangerie *f* bakery
brasserie *f* bar *(large)*
bureau *m* **de tabac** tobacconist
bus *m* bus

C

cabine *f* **(téléphonique)** telephone booth
caisse *f* cash register
car *m* motor coach
carrefour *m* intersection
carte *f* **d'identité** ID
caution *f* deposit; security
Cédez le passage! Yield!
centre *m* center
change *m* money exchange
charcuterie *f* cold cuts
chaud warm; hot
chaussée *f* road(way)
chèque *m* check
cinéma *m* cinema; movie theater
coiffeur *m* hair dresser
composter to validate
composteur *m* validation machine *(for tickets)*
compris included
contrôle *m* check *(tickets)*
croisement *m* intersection

D

dames *f/pl* ladies' room
danger *m* deanger
dangereux dangerous
déjeuner *m* lunch
départ *m* departure
déviation *f* detour
dimanche *m* Sunday

dîner *m* diner
direction *f* direction;
management
distributeur *m* **automatique**
vending machine

E

eau *f* **(non) potable** (Non)
potable water
église *f* church
enfants *m/pl* children
Entrez! Come in!
épicerie *f* grocery store
escaliers *m/pl* **roulants** escalator
essence *f* petrol; gasoline
étrangé foreign
euro *m* euro
exposition *f* exibition
extincteur *m* fire extinguisher

F

fait main handmade
femmes ladies
fermé closed
fête *f* party
feu *m* **(de signalisation)** traffic
light
foire *f* (trade) fair
français French
France *f* France
froid cold
fumer to smoke
fumeur *m* smoking; smoker

G

gardé guarded

gare *f* station; **– routière**
bus station
gazole *m* diesel
grand magasin *m* department
store
gratuit without charge
groupe *m* group
guichet *m* counter

H

halles *f/pl* indoor market
handicapés *m/pl* handicapped
hebdomadaire weekly
heures *f/pl* **d'ouverture** opening
hours
heure *f* hour
hommes *m/pl* men
hôpital *m* hospital
horaire *m* schedule
hors service not in service
hôtel *m* hotel; **– de ville** city hall

I

impair odd *(number)*
ici here
inclus included
information *f* information
interdit prohibited
issue *f* **de secours** emergency exit

J

jeudi *m* Thursday
jour *m* day; **– férié** holiday;
– ouvrable week day
journaux *m/pl* newspapers

L

laverie f **automatique**
  laundomat
lettres f/pl letters
librairie f book store
libre free; – **service** m
  self service
location f rental
lundi m Monday

M

mairie f town hall
marché m market; – **aux puces**
  flee market
mardi m Tuesday
matin m morning
médecin m physician
menu m menu
mercredi m Wednesday
Messieurs m/pl gentlemen
métro m underground; subway
monnaie f change (money)
musée m museum

N

non-fumeur m non smoking
nuit f night
numéro m number

O

objets m/pl **trouvés** lost and
  found
occupé occupied; taken
office m **de tourisme** tourist office
ouvert open

P

pair even (number)
parcmètre m parking meter
parking m parking lot
passage m **souterrain**
  underpass
passeport m passport
péage m toll; toll plaza
pension f bed & breakfast
périphérique m ring road
petit déjeuner m breakfast
pharmacie f pharmacy
pièce f coin
piéton m pedestrian
piscine f public pool
place f square
plat m **du jour** daily menu
poids m **lourd** truck
police f police
pont m bridge
port m harbor
poste f mail; post office; –
  restante in care of (mail)
Poussez! Push!
premier first
premiers secours m/pl first aid
pressing m dry cleaner
priorité f right of way
prix m price
privé private
prochain next
promotion f on sale
Prudence! f Caution!
P.T.T. f/pl (Postes, télégraphe
  et téléphone) mail and
  telephone
public public

R

ralentir to drive slowly
réception f reception
réclamation f complaint
réduction f reduction
réduit reduced
renseignements m/pl information
R.E.R. m (réseau express
  régional) local train
restaurant m restaurant
retard m delay
rez-de-chaussée m ground floor
Risque m d'incendie fire risk

S

salle f hall; – d'attente waiting
  room
Salut! Hi!
samedi m Saturday
S.A.M.U. m (Service d'aide
  médicale urgente) emergency
  service
seconde f second (time)
service m service (restaurant)
signature f signature
Silence! Silence, please!
S.N.C.F. f (Société nationale
  des chemins de fer français)
  French railway service
soir m evening
sonner to ring
sonnette f door bell
sortie f exit
sous-sol m basement
station f de métro
  underground/subway station

Stationnement m réglementé!
  Prking with permit only!
Suisse f Switzerland
Syndicat m d'initiative tourist
  office

T

tabac m tobacco store
Tarif m des consommations price
  list (in bar/restaurant)
téléphone m telephone
terrain m de camping campgro-
  und
T.G.V. m (train à grande vitesse)
  high speed train
théâtre m theater
ticket m ticket
timbres m/pl stamps
Tirez! Pull!
Toilettes f/pl restrooms
tous les jours (sauf) daily (except)
tout droit straight ahead
toutes directions all directions

V

vendredi m Friday
vente f sale
visite f tour; – guidée guided tour

Z

zone f piétonne pedestrian zone